"Matt Bell's book is a must-read for everyone desiring greater economic stability and improved financial health, especially in a difficult economy. The sound, biblically based principles presented in *Money Strategies for Tough Times* may be the difference between thriving and merely surviving the current financial turmoil."

—DAVE BRIGGS, director, Good $ense, Willow Creek Community Church

"In the current downturn many are looking for realistic, practical solutions. If you are in a financial crunch or crisis, or just wanting to avoid either of these possibilities, Matt Bell's new book *Money Strategies for Tough Times* is for you. It is filled with timely, current, and relevant help for the needs and realities of today."

—DAVE TRAVIS, managing director, Leadership Network

"Are you concerned about your financial future? Do you know someone struggling financially? Matt Bell's book gives solid advice, proven answers, and great website resources to help anyone in a tough place financially to move to higher ground."

—DR. BRIAN KLUTH, author of *40 Day Generous Life*,
radio speaker, www.GiveWithJoy.org

"Despite all the fear and uncertainty that characterizes our economy these days, one fact is certain: God is in control and has given us timeless wisdom to navigate these difficult financial times. Matt Bell has written a timely book with practical tools that will help us apply biblical wisdom to any financial difficulties."

—GUNNAR JOHNSON,
executive pastor of financial stewardship ministries, Gateway Church

"Many of us have strolled through life with too little thought given to money strategies—until now. The current economic crisis has driven everyone, from the simplest to the savviest, to reevaluate their financial plans. People are looking for anything to bring stability to their finances in the midst of the current storm. Fortunately, there is hope. In Matt's clear and practical fashion, he outlines steps and gives answers that will guide you out and keep you out of whatever financial trap you may find yourself in."

—JONATHAN MASTERS, executive pastor, Park Community Church

"If I had to choose one book to help weather the financial crisis we are in, it would be *Money Strategies for Tough Times*. In this day and age, when we're bombarded with financial advice, what I love about Matt's strategies is that they are practical, based on expertise, and, most important, biblical. A must-read for anyone serious about financial freedom."

—ASHLEY WOOLDRIDGE, executive pastor, Christ's Church of the Valley

Matt Bell's

MONEY STRATEGIES FOR TOUGH TIMES

- Get Past the Crisis • Find Some Breathing Space
- Ditch the Debt • Position Yourself for Lasting Success

Willow Creek Resources

NAVPRESS⊘.

NavPress is the publishing ministry of The Navigators, an international Christian organization and leader in personal spiritual development. NavPress is committed to helping people grow spiritually and enjoy lives of meaning and hope through personal and group resources that are biblically rooted, culturally relevant, and highly practical.

For a free catalog go to www.NavPress.com
or call 1.800.366.7788 in the United States or 1.800.839.4769 in Canada.

ISBN: 978-1-60006-664-1
Cover design by Arvid Wallen
Cover photo by Alexander Garcia

Published in association with the literary agency of Wolgemuth & Associates, Inc.

This book is designed to provide accurate and authoritative information in regard to the subject matter covered. It is sold with the understanding that neither the author nor the publisher is engaged in rendering legal, accounting, or other professional services. If legal advice or other professional advice, including financial, is required, the services of a competent professional person should be sought. The author and publisher specifically disclaim any and all liability arising directly or indirectly from the use or application of any information contained in this book. Some of the anecdotal illustrations in this book are true to life and are included with the permission of the persons involved. All other illustrations are composites of real situations, and any resemblance to people living or dead is coincidental.

Some of the anecdotal illustrations in this book are true to life and are included with the permission of the persons involved. All other illustrations are composites of real situations, and any resemblance to people living or dead is coincidental.

Unless otherwise identified, all Scripture quotations in this publication are taken from the *Holy Bible, New International Version*® (NIV®). Copyright © 1973, 1978, 1984 by International Bible Society. Used by permission of Zondervan. All rights reserved. Other versions used include: the New American Standard Bible® (NASB), Copyright © 1960, 1962, 1963, 1968, 1971, 1972, 1973, 1975, 1977, 1995 by The Lockman Foundation. Used by permission; the New King James Version (NKJV). Copyright © 1982 by Thomas Nelson, Inc. Used by permission. All rights reserved; *The Holy Bible, New Century Version* copyright © 1987, 1988, 1991 by Word Publishing, Dallas, Texas 75039. Used by permission; and the *Holy Bible*, New Living Translation (NLT), copyright © 1996. Used by permission of Tyndale House Publishers, Inc., Wheaton, Illinois 60189. All rights reserved.

Library of Congress Cataloging-in-Publication Data

Bell, Matt, 1960-
  Matt Bell's money strategies for tough times : ditch the debt, get past the crisis, find some breathing space, position yourself for lasting success / Matt Bell.
       p. cm. -- (Matt Bell's money strategies for tough times)
  Includes bibliographical references and index.
  ISBN 978-1-60006-664-1 (alk. paper)
  1. Finance, Personal. 2. Finance, Personal--Religious aspects--Christianity. I. Title. II. Title: Money strategies for tough times.
  HG179.B3725 2009
  332.024--dc22
                          2008055587

Printed in the United States of America

1 2 3 4 5 6 7 8 / 13 12 11 10 09

This book is dedicated to the memory of my parents, Jerry and Louise Bell.

They were there for me during my financial tough times — and always.

CONTENTS

Chapter 1

You *Can* Get to a Better Place

Hope is a good thing, maybe the best of things.

— ANDY DUFRESNE, *THE SHAWSHANK REDEMPTION*

When Jesus warned his disciples, "In this world you will have trouble" (John 16:33), he demonstrated that he is not just master of the universe but also master of the understatement. His concern was about the persecution his followers would face because of their faith. But there's plenty of other trouble we can get into in this world, much of which has to do with money.

Because you're reading this book, it's likely you're in the midst of some financial trouble. Maybe you're struggling to pay your credit card or medical bills. Perhaps you've gotten behind on a student loan, your taxes, or your mortgage. Maybe you've lost your job or you're fearful about a turbulent economy. I'll address each of these issues and more in the chapters that follow, giving you the practical solutions and encouragement you need to get to a better place—and stay there.

This book differs from other books about dealing with financial problems in two important ways. First, it's not about quick-fix solutions to your problems; it's about getting through the tough times with solutions that will last. Second, it comes at the conversation from a biblical perspective. Tough times call for timeless principles, and the principles taught in God's Word have stood for thousands of years. You'll find them highly relevant and deeply encouraging.

As a case in point, right after Jesus warned his friends about the problems they would likely face, he added these strong words of hope: "But take heart! I have overcome the world" (John 16:33). His assurance is that he will always be with us and that even in the midst of difficult circumstances, we can experience peace through our relationship with him.

Before starting the process of overcoming your financial problems, I'd like you to focus on four timeless truths from God's Word and come up with a compelling vision that will sustain you as you do the work that lies ahead.

Take In These Words of Encouragement

God Cares

You might think God is too busy to be bothered with your financial problems. Maybe you imagine him saying, "Behind on your bills? Hey, I've got wars and famines to deal with. Go figure this one out on your own." But listen to his invitation: "Come to me, all you who are weary and burdened, and I will give you rest. Take my yoke upon you and learn from me, for I am gentle and humble in heart, and you will find rest for your souls. For my yoke is easy and my burden is light" (Matthew 11:28-30).

Jesus didn't say, "Come to me, those of you who have exhausted every other option." He said, "Come to me *all* you who are weary and burdened." Now read it one more time, only this time fill in your name, "Come to me, _____, and I will give you rest. Take my yoke upon you and learn from me, for I am gentle and humble in heart, and you will find rest for your souls. For my yoke is easy and my burden is light."

This stunning invitation isn't from some advice peddler on a late-night television infomercial who is imploring you to come to his workshop; it's from the God of the universe, and he is inviting you to come to *him*!

In a similar passage, the apostle Peter tells us, "Cast all your anxiety on him because he cares for you" (1 Peter 5:7). There's that word *all* again. Don't just bring *some* of your concerns to God; bring every one of them. He wants you to come to him with your worries about losing your home, finding a job, or recovering from losses in your retirement plan. He wants you to come to him with your fears, discouragement, questions, and anger. He wants you to come, just as you are. If you're wondering whether he's even there in the midst of your troubles, he wants you to come to him with your doubts.

That the God of the universe cares about us is one of the most amazing and encouraging promises of Scripture. God knows all the details of your life; he knows the stresses on your mind and the fears in your heart. He knows your needs, and he *promises* to provide for you (see Matthew 6:25-34).

Others Can Help

We were designed for community, and that's especially true when we're facing tough times. The Bible says,

> Two are better than one,
>   because they have a good return for their work:
> If one falls down,
>   his friend can help him up.
> But pity the man who falls
>   and has no one to help him up! (Ecclesiastes 4:9-10)

When the going gets tough, some of us go into hiding. We don't want to burden others with our problems. We don't want others to even know that we have problems. But it's during times of trouble when we need community the most.

I once had twenty thousand dollars of credit card debt. In a classic prodigal son reenactment, I inherited sixty thousand from an uncle, spent it all and twenty thousand more trying to create my dream job and fund an increasingly expensive lifestyle, and then moved home with my parents for six months so I could start climbing out of debt. About a year after moving out on my own again, while working as a freelance radio journalist, I felt as if my radio career had gone as far as it could go. One Sunday night, I flipped open the job listings in the *Chicago Tribune*, saw an ad for a position perfectly suited to my audio production skills, sent in a résumé, and got the job. It was a good move in many ways, particularly because of the steady income and insurance benefits it provided.

About five years into that job, my relationship with my boss soured and I negotiated a deal whereby I became an independent contractor for the company, responsible for selling a line of audio training products I helped develop. It didn't go well. Soon I found myself looking at job listings again, feeling much less certain about what type of work to pursue. I was directionless and discouraged. I was out of credit card debt, but I knew if I didn't find a job soon I could easily slip right back into debt. An image kept coming to mind of me sitting on top of a high thin wall feeling as if I could tumble off at any moment and just fall and fall. I was getting scared.

I was also getting angry with God. Hadn't I gone through enough? Why would he allow me to go through another tough time with money? I was meeting with a group of friends every Friday night to run and study the Bible together. I remember one get-together when I was in an especially foul mood. The minute one of the guys suggested that we pray, my irritated reply was, "Yeah, right." We did, indeed, pray that night—and many other nights. Sometimes I was angry, sometimes indifferent; other times I was barely there. But we prayed, which would not have been the case had I been alone. I had fallen down in my faith, yet my friends helped me up.

Yours can too.

Nothing Is Impossible with God, So Pray Big

When I became involved in a national financial ministry called Good $ense, I was introduced to the concept of "God's math." There's a lot of calculator work involved in managing money and helping others with their finances, but God's involvement in our finances often transcends the world of addition, subtraction, and balanced budgets. God can—and he just might—deliver you from your financial problems. There are examples in Scripture of God doing so, such as this account from 2 Kings 4:1-7.

The wife of a man from the company of the prophets cried out to Elisha, "Your servant my husband is dead, and you know that he revered the LORD. But now his creditor is coming to take my two boys as his slaves."

Elisha replied to her, "How can I help you? Tell me, what do you have in your house?"

"Your servant has nothing there at all," she said, "except a little oil."

Elisha said, "Go around and ask all your neighbors for empty jars. Don't ask for just a few. Then go inside and shut the door behind you and your sons. Pour oil into all the jars, and as each is filled, put it to one side."

She left him and afterward shut the door behind her and her sons. They brought the jars to her and she kept pouring. When all the jars were full, she said to her son, "Bring me another one."

But he replied, "There is not a jar left." Then the oil stopped flowing.

She went and told the man of God, and he said, "Go, sell the oil and pay your debts. You and your sons can live on what is left."

God enabled the prophet Elisha to perform a miracle that delivered this woman from her debts. Indeed, "nothing is impossible with God" (Luke 1:37). God still does miracles. Do you believe that?

I recently met with someone who has more than eighty thousand dollars of student loans. He is resigned to never being able to pay it off—to making payments on that debt for the rest of his life. But it doesn't necessarily have to be that way.

Part of the solution to this young man's discouragement is knowledge. As we will discuss in chapter 4, those with federally subsidized student loans may be eligible to have their balance wiped out after making payments for a certain amount of years (it's not a short amount of time, but it's certainly shorter than the average life span!).

In addition to knowledge, this man needed faith that God would help him find a solution for paying back his debt. So do you. I'm not encouraging you to have blind faith or to casually say, "God will provide," while not *doing* anything about your situation. But I am encouraging you to trust that God will meet you in your difficulties in ways you can't possibly imagine. Maybe he will bring an unexpected windfall into your life. Perhaps he will orchestrate the forgiveness of your debts. Maybe in the midst of your troubles, he will give you a peace that surpasses understanding.

God Has a Purpose for What You're Going Through

However long it takes to resolve your financial issues, rest assured that God has a purpose for your tough times. While Scripture contains examples of his immediately solving people's problems, it also tells of people praying for a remedy without finding quick answers. That doesn't mean God doesn't care. It certainly doesn't mean he isn't with you in your troubles. God promised to be with us *always* (see Joshua 1:5). It may simply mean that your preferred schedule for the relief of your problems is not the schedule he has in mind. As a wise person once said, "God is rarely early, but he's never late."

Think of the apostle Paul. He asked God again and again for relief from some unspecified thorn in his flesh. Whatever his difficulty was, it was such an issue for him that he referred to it as no less than "a messenger of Satan" (2 Corinthians 12:7), yet God kept telling him to trust.

Three times I pleaded with the Lord to take it away from me. But he said to me, "My grace is sufficient for you, for my power is made perfect in weakness." Therefore I will boast all the more gladly about my weaknesses, so that Christ's power may rest on me. That is why, for Christ's sake, I delight in weaknesses, in insults, in hardships, in persecutions, in difficulties. For when I am weak, then I am strong. (12:8-10)

The notion that God's power is made perfect in my weakness resonated with me when I was digging my way out of debt. God was using the pain of my financial problems to draw me closer to him. He wanted me to understand my utter dependence on him and to accept that he loves me and is watching over me. God did not cause my problems, but he brought purpose and meaning in the midst of them. While I was eager to get out of debt quickly, it took those four and a half years for God to begin reshaping some of my assumptions about what matters and to mold my heart and character.

What do you sense God wants you to learn from your situation? Take a minute and jot down a few thoughts here. Then, from time to time, come back to what you wrote and add any new insights that come to mind.

_____

_____

_____

_____

_____

_____

As you look for the larger purpose in your situation, trust this: "We know that in all things God works for the good of those who love him, who have been called according to his purpose" (Romans 8:28). God uses *all* things for good, including your financial difficulties.

If you are going through tough times, you need encouragement. To help you persevere and give you hope, remind yourself often of these four, key truths: God cares; others can help; nothing is impossible with God, so pray big; and God has a purpose for what you're going through.

And raise your sights. Let me explain.

Make No Little Plans

As a Chicagoan, I've long been drawn to a quote attributed to Daniel Burnham, the visionary architect and city planner who designed Chicago's beautiful open lakefront in the early 1900s. He said, "Make no little plans. They have no magic to stir men's blood."

Why do you want to solve the financial problems you are facing? You may be thinking, *Well, isn't it obvious? I have creditors hounding me. I want them off my back!*

That's a natural response. When we're in pain, relieving that pain becomes our overriding goal. But I want you to think bigger. Paul reminded us that we follow a big God:

No eye has seen,
    no ear has heard,
no mind has conceived
    what God has prepared for those who love him.
(1 Corinthians 2:9)

What might you be able to do if you resolved your financial problems once and for all?

For Joe, the initial answer to this question had to do with restoring his relationship with his wife and daughters. Ultimately, his journey out of financial problems led to a far better relationship with them and with God.

Soon after getting married, he and Dawn bought a house and filled the kitchen with new appliances purchased with store financing that required no money down and no interest for twelve months. When they failed to make the final payment on time, they were socked with back interest totaling hundreds of dollars. That was the beginning of a downward financial spiral. In their second year of marriage they had their first child, and fifteen months later they had another. Complications during the second pregnancy followed by a premature birth led to thousands of dollars of medical debt.

Joe took primary responsibility for their bills, and the tighter their finances became, the more he leaned on credit cards, using one to pay the minimum due on another. When the credit cards got maxed out, he turned to payday loans (short-term, high-interest loans to cover expenses until the borrower's next payday), sometimes holding three or four at a time, which only compounded their financial problems. Joe's insurance sales job was 100 percent commission. As the weight of their financial problems led him into depression, he slept more and earned less. It got worse from there. Joe and Dawn got two months behind on their mortgage and had their utilities turned off more than once. Calls from bill collectors became more frequent, and so did their arguments.

In May, when they hit a financial low point, they had debts totaling more than $50,000 ($37,000 of credit card debts, $17,000 of medical bills, and some back taxes), their minimum monthly payments had grown to $1,600, while their monthly income had shrunk to $2,600.

They also hit an emotional low point. During an especially heated fight, Joe told Dawn to get out. Weeks passed. When Joe finally called and asked Dawn to come home, she refused. Neither one wanted a divorce, but Dawn told Joe she would not come home until their debts were paid in full.

The experience brought Joe to his knees and then to the office of a nearby pastor. "That pastor did a great thing," Joe said. "He was able to discern that our situation was not beyond our control. We had just made lots of bad decisions. He said, 'You have to get off your duff.' That was a jolt to me. I was not expecting to hear that. I was looking for sympathy. He gave me a counselor's name and said I needed to work it out."

That one-two punch got Joe moving. "When Dawn drew that line, I was very driven to get the debt paid off. It was so lonely to be home, so I worked all the time. I did everything I could to drive my commissions up and my expenses down. I shut off everything—cable, telephone. I got down to the bare necessities. I was eating sixty-nine-cent cans of vegetables."

Even though Dawn and Joe had both grown up in churchgoing families, church had not been part of their marriage. But their separation led both of them to church, and they began growing in their faith. They also took part in individual counseling, and in February of the next year, Dawn agreed to go see a counselor with Joe, which she says was "like dating again." That Thanksgiving, she and the girls moved back in with Joe. All the debts were not gone, but Dawn could see that Joe was making great progress.

"We would have easily qualified for bankruptcy," Joe said. "But when I was ready to pay the debt, I wanted to pay it all."

Joe said that prior to his separation from Dawn, he had been keeping his spiritual life and his financial life in separate compartments, but no longer. "I remember kneeling by the bed and saying, 'God, I turn these problems over to you.' I told him, 'This is my responsibility, but I need your help. I'm a trustee with what you've given me. I want to make it right.'"

It took three and a half years for Joe and Dawn to pay off their credit card, medical, and tax debts. Today the only debt they have is a mortgage, and their marriage has never been stronger.

As Joe thinks back on all that he and Dawn went through, he says that Isaiah 42:3 sums it up best: "He will not crush those who are weak or quench the smallest hope" (NLT).[1]

What about you? What hope has God placed on your heart? Maybe your marriage isn't on the brink of divorce, but is it all that it could be? Would resolving your financial issues help you resolve some festering stress in your relationship? Would getting past your money problems help you pursue that career move that's been tugging at your heart for so long—the one that seems so unrealistic, so impossible? Would getting to a better place with your finances enable you to help your children graduate from college without debt or free you to give more generously to a cause you believe in? If finances weren't an issue, what dreams could you fulfill? As followers of Christ, we too are taught to make no little plans. The Bible says that God is able to do "immeasurably more than all we ask or imagine" (Ephesians 3:20). What no-little-plans dream has God given you? Write down what comes to mind:

_____

_____

_____

_____

Doesn't that feel more exciting than just solving your financial problems? Can you feel your blood starting to stir? Can you sense God's delight?

_____

_____

_____

Daniel Burnham left a shimmering legacy to all who live in or visit Chicago: a beautiful park-lined lakefront that every year draws countless picnickers, bikers, runners, and strollers. The goal you're able to pursue by first resolving your financial problems could be a powerful part of your legacy as well.

Renew Your Mind, Encourage Your Heart

In the chapters that follow, there will be no shortage of action steps for getting out of financial trouble. I certainly want you to take action. But I also want to encourage you to lean on Christ as never before. In a famous passage of Scripture, James stressed the need for both faith *and* action.

> Suppose a brother or sister is without clothes and daily food. If one of you says to him, "Go, I wish you well; keep warm and well fed," but does nothing about his physical needs, what good is it? In the same way, faith by itself, if it is not accompanied by action, is dead. (James 2:15-17)

James' concern was that people might err too much on the side of faith. Mine is just the opposite. Don't just follow the action steps in this book. Take time to let the Scripture at the end of each chapter soak in so that God's Word can renew your mind and encourage your heart.

Now turn the page and get started on your journey out of the tough times.

Chapter 2

You Are Here

The first step towards getting somewhere is to decide that
you are not going to stay where you are.

— JOHN PIERPONT MORGAN

We live fairly close to a sprawling outdoor mall. I've been there
many times, and yet it never gets any easier to find my way
around. My first stop is always the nearest mall map, where I look
for the red "You are here" dot in order to plot a course to where I'm
going.

In order to get to where you want to be with your finances, you too
need to be clear about where you are right now.

You may prefer not to know how bad things really are. That's
normal. You've probably had the experience of slicing up an apple and
accidentally cutting your finger in the process. As you held the finger
with your other hand, you might not have looked at the cut because
you were afraid of how bad the cut might be.

Of course, the only way to fix a problem—whether it's bleeding
fingers or bleeding finances—is to assess how bad it is. But you have
to go even further than that: You also have to determine what caused
the problem. Otherwise, you'll just patch things up, only to face the
same problem again and again. In order to get out of debt—and stay
there—you need to get clear about the magnitude of your financial
problems and how they came about.

When you get clarity about your financial problems, you'll come to one of two conclusions: Either you are in a true financial crisis or you are merely in a financial crunch. Many people who believe they are in a crisis are actually in a crunch, for which many solutions are available. Of course, you may discover that you are, in fact, in a true crisis. Even so, if you are serious about getting your finances in order, you can do so.

Either way, it's essential that you find out where you are right now. That knowledge will put you in a position of strength from which you can move to a better place, so let's get started.

Totaling Up Your Debts

The following *Debt Organizer* can help you get a handle on how much you owe. On the left side, list each of your creditors: credit cards on which you carry a balance, vehicle loans, student loans, medical debts, tax debts, personal loans, loans against a retirement account such as a 401(k) or 403(b) plan, and any other debts, with the exception of your mortgage (we'll focus on solutions to mortgage issues in chapter 5).

Now enter the total balance for each debt, the interest rate, and the monthly payment amount. Don't guess at this; pull out your most recent statements and gather the facts. Last, indicate whether you are current on each debt—that is, whether you've made your most recent payment by the due date.

Getting Organized

Debt and disorganization seem to go together. Maybe it's part of the denial process; keeping files scattered is one way to avoid facing how bad things are. Unfortunately, it's also a good way to stay stuck in a financial quagmire. In order to move to a better place with your finances, get organized.

Buy some file folders and dedicate a desk drawer to your financial life. Group your folders in five sections in the following order: income,

Debt Organizer

Creditor	Total Balance	Interest Rate	Monthly Payment Amount	Current? Yes/No
Total		N/A		N/A

generosity, savings/investments, debts (credit cards, student loans, vehicle loans, and so on), and other monthly bills (keep the folder for your mortgage here, in the "Other Monthly Bills" section, along with folders for utilities, insurance, and so forth). In the "Income" section, have a distinct pay-stubs folder for each source of income you have. If you use more than one bank, use a separate folder in the "Savings/Investments" section for each one. If you donate money to multiple organizations, use a separate folder for each one in the "Generosity" section. You get the idea.

Now take two additional steps with each folder in the "Debts" section. First, in the top left portion of the front of the folder, write which month we're in right now. To the right of that, write the current total balance, and to the right of that, write this month's minimum required payment. For example:

Month	Balance	Minimum Payment
April	$2,595.26	$52

Each month, add a new line, starting with the month and then the new totals. This will help you track your progress in paying off your debts. Arrange the file folders so that the debt with the lowest balance is the first one, moving progressively to the highest-balance debt. If you can find some money to add to the minimum required payments, apply the extra amount to your lowest-balance debt first. (We'll talk more about how to do this in the next chapter.)

Pay close attention to each of your bills. If you pay bills electronically, print your statements each month for at least a year. Before filing them, compare them with the previous month's statements. By doing this, you're more likely to catch any billing mistakes and you may be prompted to consider options for lowering or even eliminating some bills. For example, just paying closer attention to your electric and gas bills may motivate you to take steps to manage your use of electricity and gas more proactively.

Now let's get a handle on your monthly income versus expenses.

Totaling Up Your Cash Flow

Fill in as best you can both of the "Now" columns on the *Monthly Cash Flow Plan* on page 27. You can print additional forms that might be easier to work with from my website (go to www.moneypurpose joy.com and click on the "Resources" tab). The "Now" figures should reflect your current situation, not what you believe you ought to be doing or what you hope to do.

Start with your gross monthly income—the amount you receive each month before any deductions are taken from your check for taxes, insurance, retirement plan savings, or anything else. If you are paid every two weeks (as opposed to twice a month), take the amount you are paid each paycheck, multiply the amount by twenty-six, divide by twelve, and enter that amount. That's your true monthly income.

Next, if you give away some money each month, enter that amount.

Then fill in how much you are saving each month. If you are contributing a set amount each month to an emergency fund, what I call an *If* savings account (as in *If you lose your job . . .*), put that amount on the *If* line. Near-term *When* savings are for goals you are saving toward that you'd like to accomplish within the next five years. Mid-term *When* savings are for goals you'd like to accomplish in the next five to ten years. Long-term *When* savings are any amounts you're setting aside each month for your retirement or a child's college costs. *Why* savings are for any special dreams you're pursuing. (We'll discuss these types of savings in more detail in chapter 8.)

Now fill in the amounts you're paying on the debts you listed in your *Debt Organizer*.

Next, as best you can, fill in the monthly amount you are spending in each of the remaining categories. You may need to guess at some of the figures, which is fine for now. Remember, if you are paid every two weeks and items such as taxes, medical insurance, and retirement plan savings are deducted from your paycheck, take each amount, multiply by twenty-six, divide by twelve, and enter that amount. Also, keep in mind that you might not spend money every month in some categories. Examples include real estate taxes, insurance bills that you pay on a semi-annual or annual basis, gifts, vacations, and home and car maintenance. Estimate how much you spend in these categories on an annual basis, divide by twelve, and enter those amounts.

Last, fill in your total monthly income, total monthly expenses, and total monthly income minus total monthly expenses.

You may find that you have more expenses than income. That's okay—for now. Remember, the point of this exercise is to get at the truth of your current situation. In the next chapter, I'll take you through numerous ways to turn your situation around so that you have more income than expenses.

Getting Clear About Your Cash Flow

So far, you have *estimated* your monthly cash flow. That's a great start. Now we need to go further and make the numbers as accurate as possible. Do so by tracking all of your income and expenses using the *Monthly Cash Flow Tracker* on pages 28–29. This may be a new discipline for you, but trust me on this: If you get yourself in the habit of tracking your income and expenses, you will find the information so helpful and freeing that you'll wonder why you ever resisted the idea.

Tracking your income and expenses and then using the information to proactively *manage* your money are two of the most powerful steps you can take to get past a crisis and out of debt. These steps will help you find some breathing space and position yourself for lasting success. Build these habits and you will give yourself the best possible chance of getting to a better place with your finances and staying there.

Just hang on to the receipts for anything you buy each day or jot down what you paid. At the end of each day, write your expenses in the appropriate categories in the *Monthly Cash Flow Tracker.* This should take just a few minutes every day. Wondering what category a certain expense goes in, such as that coffee you bought on the way to work? Let's see, should it be "Food" or "Entertainment"? You decide. The important thing is that you capture all of your spending each day. Don't worry about the row marked "Goals" right now. For now just get in the habit of recording your income and expenses.

Capture everything: the amount you spent on train fare, lunch, dry cleaning, and so on. When you receive a paycheck, enter the total amount before any deductions are taken. Then enter the various deductions in the appropriate categories. If money is taken out for a retirement savings plan, enter that amount in "Saving/Investing." Put the total amount taken out for taxes, Social Security, and Medicare in

Monthly Cash Flow Plan

	Now	Goal		Now	Goal
Monthly Income			**Income Taxes**		
Salary 1 (gross)			Federal		
Salary 2 (gross)			State		
Other			Social Security (FICA)		
			Medicare		
Giving			Other		
Church					
Other			**Food**		
			Clothing		
Saving/Investing					
If (emergency fund)			**Household/Personal**		
When (near-term)			Dry cleaning		
When (mid-term)			Gifts		
When (long-term)			Furniture/household		
Why (dreams)			Cosmetics		
			Barber/beauty		
Consumer Debts			Allowances		
Credit card			Education		
Credit card					
Credit card			**Entertainment**		
Vehicle			Restaurants/movies		
Education			Cable/satellite TV		
Other			Vacations		
			Books/subscriptions		
Housing			Health club/hobbies		
Mortgage/rent			Pets		
Real estate tax					
Insurance			**Health**		
			Medical/dental insurance		
Maintenance/Utilities			Prescriptions/co-pays		
Maintenance			HSA/FSA		
Electric			Disability insurance		
Gas			Life insurance		
Water					
Garbage			**Professional Services**		
Home phone/Internet			Legal/accounting		
Cell phone			Counseling		
			Child care/babysitting		
Transportation					
Gas			**Miscellaneous**		
Maintenance					
Insurance			**Total Monthly Income**		
Bus/train/parking/tolls			**Total Monthly Expenses**		
License/fees			**Income Minus Expenses**		

Monthly Cash Flow Tracker

	Income	Giving	Saving/ Investing	Debts	Mort./Rent, Real Estate Tax, Ins.	Home Maint./ Utilities	Transp.
Goals ⟶							
Total							
(Over)/ Under							
Last Month's YTD							
Total YTD							

1	2	3	4	5	6	7	8	9	10	11	12	13	14	15

Month _____

| Income Taxes | Food | Clothing | Household/Personal | | | Enter-tainment | Health | Prof. Svcs. | Misc. |
			Gifts	Beauty/ Barber	All Other				

| 16 | 17 | 18 | 19 | 20 | 21 | 22 | 23 | 24 | 25 | 26 | 27 | 28 | 29 | 30 | 31 |

"Income Taxes." Enter the amount taken out for medical, disability, and dental insurance in "Health." I want you to enter your *gross* income and then itemize all of the deductions because some of the deductions are not as fixed as you might think; they're manageable. I'll say more about that in the next chapter.

The numbers at the bottom of the form are some of the most important numbers on the *Monthly Cash Flow Tracker*. They are the days of the month. After you enter your spending for a certain day, cross through that date as a reminder that you've captured that day's expenses. This habit of recording each day's expenses is essential if you are to have accurate information from which you can plan future spending.

The space underneath "Goals" is for whatever notes you may want to make about your expenses, such as who you bought a gift for or what clothing you bought.

Knowing Your Credit Score

One other number I'd like you to know is your credit score. You can get your credit *report* from each of the three credit bureaus once a year for free through the website www.annualcreditreport.com. Your credit *score*, however, is not free. Just to make matters a bit confusing, you have a different score at each bureau, although they should be similar. For now, just buy your score from Equifax. It's the only one of the three that offers the FICO credit score, a widely used score developed by Fair Isaac Corporation (that's where FICO comes from). You'll be able to order the score during the process of obtaining your credit reports. It should cost less than ten dollars.

Credit scores range from 300 to 850; the higher the better.

If You Are in a True Financial Crisis . . .

So what do you think? Are you in a financial crisis or a financial crunch? Most people who are experiencing financial difficulties are in a financial crunch, not crisis. Even if your estimated expenses are higher than your income, I wouldn't necessarily call that a crisis. There are numerous ways to flip the equation so that your income is higher than your expenses.

However, you might truly be in a financial crisis. That means that your health or home is at risk because your expenses are so much higher than your income that you are falling behind on certain essential bills. Examples include: not being able to afford your rent or mortgage, utilities, food, or medical care; or being threatened with lawsuits or wage garnishment.

If you are in a financial crisis, you need to distinguish your essential bills from those that are less essential. If you don't have enough money to meet your expenses this month, take care of your most important needs first. You need a place to live, food to eat, utilities, and medical care. These bills need to be your priorities, which may mean paying bills other than the ones that bill collectors are calling you about.

See how much money you have in a checking or savings account, estimate how much income you'll be able to generate over the next couple of months, and then, using your *Monthly Cash Flow Plan*, total up how much money you need for the next couple of months for housing, food, utilities, and any needed medical care.

Next, write down here what you are doing to remedy your situation. For example, if you're out of work, are you applying for jobs? If you're working but can't pay all your bills, are you looking for an additional part-time job? Anyone that you turn to for help has a right to know the answers to these questions.

_____

_____

_____

_____

_____

_____

_____

_____

If you need immediate financial help, here are some ideas for where to go:

Family Members or Friends

Is there a family member or friend you could live with or someone who might loan or give you enough money to meet your immediate needs?

Your Church

There is a biblical mandate to provide for other believers. First John 3:17 states, "If anyone has material possessions and sees his brother in need but has no pity on him, how can the love of God be in him?" The model of the early church was to share so that other believers were not in need (see Acts 4:32-35). Your church may have a benevolence program specifically designed to help meet the needs of the members of the congregation or community.

A Nearby Food Bank

If family and friends and your church can't help and you do not have enough money for food, this is a viable option. If you've never been to a food bank before, it may be difficult to work up the nerve to go. Keep in mind that they exist to help people who are temporarily unable to afford food. Far better to go to a food bank than go without food. Feeding America, formerly known as America's Second Harvest, is a national food bank network. On their site, www.feedingamerica.org, you will find a food bank locator.

Additional Sources of Assistance

Many hospitals and doctors' offices make free medical care available to those unable to pay. If you need medical help, call a nearby medical facility and ask to speak to someone in the financial aid department or check their website. Various government benefits are available for people in need. Go to www.govbenefits.gov to find aid programs for which you may qualify. Another option is an organization called Modest Needs (www.modestneeds.org), which provides grants for families facing temporary financial difficulties.

All of the above-mentioned solutions should be viewed as short-term ones. They are places to turn to make sure you have somewhere to live, utilities, food to eat, and medical care for the immediate future. The chapters that follow will help you regain control of your financial situation so that you can become self-sufficient as soon as possible.

Once you've identified where you are, it's also important to acknowledge how you got there.

How Did You Get Here?

If you are to get to a better place with your finances and *stay there*, you must deal with the root causes of your financial problems. Look at the following circumstances and check off each one that contributed to your situation:

- ☐ Unemployment
- ☐ Death of a spouse
- ☐ An addiction to drugs, alcohol, pornography, or gambling
- ☐ Medical bills
- ☐ Divorce
- ☐ Small-business failure
- ☐ Living beyond my means

Did you include that last option? You might have gone through some horrendous experiences, and your circumstances may, in fact, be completely beyond your control. Companies downsize and lay off many people at a time. Medical bills can easily get out of hand, even for those with insurance. After many years of leading financial workshops, I've learned that no matter what circumstances may have contributed to a person's financial tough times, most people also acknowledge some degree of personal responsibility for their situation. It's usually about their financial habits. If they'd had savings when they lost their job, their situation wouldn't have gotten so bad so quickly. If they hadn't gotten in the habit of carrying a balance on their credit cards, the divorce might not have been quite so financially painful.

I'm not trying to add insult to injury. It's just that people with financial difficulties often look for the quickest possible fix. They may even succeed in getting out of trouble for a while. But what often happens is that people get past their immediate financial crisis only to get right back into trouble within a short period of time. That's because they treated their symptoms without getting at the root causes — especially any role that they played in their difficulties. On these lines, write down one or two new financial habits that will leave you better prepared to handle any future financial storms.

_____

_____

_____

_____

_____

Now let's take this search for the root cause of your situation a step further.

Are There Any Issues Behind the Issue?

On the surface, it looked as if the cause of Debbie's financial problems was gambling. After her husband was killed in an accident, some relatives began taking her to casinos as a way to help her get her mind off the pain of her loss. "At first it was an escape," she said, "but then I kind of got lost in it." Debbie figures that in the six years following her husband's death, she gambled away $150,000. Some of the money came from a life insurance settlement she received, but $40,000 of it went on her credit cards, and another $20,000 on a home equity loan.

A bankruptcy filing and three visits to Gamblers Anonymous followed, putting an end to her gambling. She even took the precaution of banning herself from nearby casinos, which meant that the casinos could not permit her to visit. But five years after filing for bankruptcy, while vacationing with a friend, she decided to visit another casino and was drawn back in. She quickly racked up $25,000 in new debts, fueled in part by payday loans.

The situation came to a head after an all-night gambling binge. At five in the morning, she had what she calls "a revelation," losing all desire to gamble. "I was so ashamed of what I was doing. I was hiding it from people. I said, 'I can't do this anymore. Lord, you have to help me.' My life changed at that moment."

Debbie's niece introduced her to John, the head of a financial ministry at her church. John helped Debbie put together a budget and a plan for paying off her debts. At the same time, she began seeing a therapist. Through those counseling sessions, she had an unexpected insight into her gambling problem: She didn't want the insurance settlement money from her husband's death because it reminded her that he was gone. She gambled in order to get rid of the money.

Today, motivated by a desire to live at peace and spend time enjoying her grandchildren, Debbie is on track to being debt-free in about another year.

What about you? Do you have a sense as to the root causes of your financial troubles? If not, pray the words of the psalmist:

> Search me, O GOD, and know my heart;
> test me and know my anxious thoughts.
> See if there is any offensive way in me,
> and lead me in the way everlasting. (139:23-24)

Also, ask some close friends for their thoughts. If you want to achieve long-term financial success, it's essential that you trace your present difficulties back to their original causes and begin to remedy those issues, whether unhelpful financial habits or attitudes of the heart. If you believe that an addiction may be at the root of your financial difficulties, please seek the help of a trained counselor. You may be able to get a referral through your church.

Some people are held back from getting to a better place with their finances because they are angry or bitter. Is there someone you've been blaming for your tough times? A former spouse? A former employer? Someone who contributed to your medical problems? Forgiving is far easier to talk about than to do, but it is necessary if you want to change your financial habits and get to a place of financial peace. Ask God for his help in this process.

You might even need to forgive yourself. I did. Even though my experience of squandering my inheritance led to some positive changes in my life, I continued to feel a deep sense of guilt over my mismanagement of that money.

Forgiving myself didn't come easily. What helped was being reminded that God has forgiven me of far worse things than overspending on my credit cards. God's standard is perfect holiness. Of course, it's an impossible standard to meet. Yet the Bible says that God:

does not treat us as our sins deserve
　　or repay us according to our iniquities.
For as high as the heavens are above the earth,
　　so great is his love for those who fear him;
as far as the east is from the west,
　　so far has he removed our transgressions from us.
(Psalm 103:10-12)

If God could forgive me, then surely I could forgive myself.

Is there someone you need to forgive for your financial situation? Do you need to forgive yourself? Begin the process of forgiveness today.

WRITE IT ON YOUR HEART

"I know the plans I have for you," declares the LORD, "plans to prosper you and not to harm you, plans to give you hope and a future." (Jeremiah 29:11)

Chapter 3

How Serious Are You?

Start by doing what's necessary; then do what's possible; and suddenly you are doing the impossible.

— ST. FRANCIS OF ASSISI

Legend has it that when sixteenth-century Spanish explorer and conqueror Hernán Cortés landed in Mexico in search of treasure, he ordered his men to burn the ships they had used for their journey across the ocean. He was committed to succeeding at his mission. There was no going back to Spain. No foot out the back door. No plan B. By burning the ships, Cortés and his men had to make their mission work—and they did. He and his soldiers conquered the Aztec empire and captured the treasure they were after. That may not be a lesson in civil behavior, but it's a strong lesson in commitment.

If you're serious about getting out of debt, you'll need that same level of commitment to succeed.

Burn the Ship

If you are carrying a balance on your credit cards from month to month, commit to going no further into debt. I'm not just talking about a verbal commitment; I'm talking about a "burn the ships" *act* of commitment: Cut up your credit cards. Simple as that. Not later tonight. Not tomorrow. Put this book down right now, grab some scissors, and cut up all your credit cards.

Whether you ever use credit cards again is up to you. Joe, whom you met in chapter 1, experienced so much pain due to his misuse of credit cards that he has sworn them off for life. Going without credit cards has freed Joe from his struggles with debt, which has helped him rebuild his marriage.

Ask for Support

Which of your friends know about your difficulties? Do *any* of them know? If not, think of two friends right now whom you will confide in — two friends whom you will tell about your financial problems. If you're married, each of you should tell at least one other person about your situation. Let your accountability partners know you're not looking for advice or sympathy. Explain that you are committed to getting out of debt and you simply want their support. A little encouragement wouldn't hurt either. Ask them to pray for you regularly, and arrange to meet with them at least once a month. This last step is one of the most important parts of the deal. This meeting will be for the purpose of showing your accountability partners the statements for each of your debts. Have them write down the name of each of your creditors, the amount you owe, and this month's minimum required payment. Then each month, have them update their tally.

This will be a vivid, effective form of accountability. It's also a monthly opportunity for prayer and celebration. As you see your debts going down, you'll have much to celebrate. Don't go out for a steak dinner each month, but at least take satisfaction from your progress.

Ask for Better Rates

If you've been making your credit card payments on time, call your credit card companies and ask them to lower your interest rates. In one study, more than half of all people making such calls were successful.[1]

Here's what to say: "I think I've been a good customer. I'd like to stay with you, but I really want you to lower the rate on my card. Can you help me?" If you get turned down, ask for a supervisor and repeat your request.[2] If you have received other credit card offers in the mail, mention them. It will help because the company will want to keep your business.

If you stop adding to your debt, lowering your rate will speed up the process of getting out of debt and reduce the amount you will pay in interest. However, it won't lower your monthly payment. The interest rate impacts how much of your monthly payment goes toward interest and how much toward principal. The minimum amount due each month is determined by a separate formula, usually set at between 2 and 4 percent of your balance.

So if you are struggling to make the minimum payments on your credit cards or have missed payments, instead of asking your credit card companies for a lower interest rate, ask about their hardship programs. Tell each company you are committed to paying what you owe, explain why you are having financial difficulties, and ask for some assistance. If you've been getting late fees or other fees, your balance may be growing, even if you've stopped charging on your card. Ask your credit card companies if they will remove those fees. If they agree to remove some fees, your balance should decline, which will make your minimum-required payment decline as well. Some companies have other options that might lower your payments, at least temporarily.

Fix and Roll Your Payments

If you stop charging on a credit card and make the minimum required payment each month, the amount of that required payment will decline a little each month. However, the required payment goes down so slightly that it's hard to notice, which is one reason why I had you write your current balance and minimum due on the file folders pertaining to your credit cards. If you pay this declining minimum each month, it will keep you in debt for a long time. However, if you fix your payment on the amount that's required *this* month and keep paying that amount each month, it will significantly speed up the process of getting out of debt.

The Case Against Balance Transfers

Whenever I teach workshops about getting out of debt, someone always asks about the wisdom of transferring their high-interest credit card balances to a new card offering a low or even 0 percent interest rate. This sounds like a smart idea, but watch out. It comes with numerous hidden snares. Keep in mind that making this transfer won't necessarily change the amount you have to pay each month, unless the new card bases its minimum-required payment on a lower percentage of the balance than your current card.

When considering a balance transfer, here's what to look for in the fine print:

- **Is there a transaction fee?** Some cards charge a fee based on a percentage of the transferred balance.
- **How long will the 0 percent rate be in effect?** Some cards offer the rate for only a short "introductory period."
- **What money does the low rate pertain to?** With some cards, it applies only to the transferred balance. The card company may then require you to make a minimum number of purchases with your card each month, with those purchases subject to a higher interest rate. Any payments you make each month will not apply to those new charges until you finish paying off the transferred balance. Unless you pay off the entire transferred balance and your new charges, you'll rack up interest charges.
- **What happens if you don't follow all the rules?** If you make one late payment or exceed your credit limit one time, will the company raise your rate to its standard rate or higher?

One other factor to consider is the potential impact on your credit score, that three-digit number that affects everything from your ability to get a job to how much you pay for insurance. Opening any new account gives you access to more credit, which can lower your score. Also, make sure your debt-to-available-credit ratio does not get too high. A good rule of thumb is to keep that ratio at 10 percent or below (this advice even pertains to people who pay their balance in full each month), so know what your credit limit will be on the new card and see what percentage of that limit your transferred balance will constitute.

Here's how it works. Let's say you have a $2,000 balance on a card charging 14 percent interest and requiring a monthly payment of 3 percent of your balance. This month, your minimum payment is $60. Next month, assuming you don't charge anything more, the minimum payment will be $58.90. A month later it will be $57.82. If you pay this declining minimum each month, it will take you 140 months to pay off your balance, and you'll pay $1,152 in interest.

However, if you simply keep paying this month's required minimum of $60, you'll pay off your balance in just forty-three months, and you'll pay $548 in interest. By fixing your payment on this month's minimum, you'll be out of debt in less than one-third the time and you'll cut your interest payments by more than half.

If you have multiple debts, fix your payments on each one. When one debt is paid off, take the amount you were paying on that debt and roll it into the next-lowest-balance debt. Keep doing that and you will radically speed up the process of getting out of debt.

Accelerate the Roll

You'll be out of debt even faster if you can find an additional amount to add to your minimum-required payments. In the above-mentioned example, paying $85 per month (just $25 more than the fixed minimum) will get the debt erased in twenty-eight months and will lower the amount of interest you'll pay to $352. No matter how much extra you can come up with—$10, $50, $100—apply that accelerator to the lowest balance debt. Once that debt is wiped out, roll the full amount you were paying on that debt into the next-lowest-balance debt and on and on until you are out of debt. With the help of your *Monthly Cash Flow Plan*, along with the ideas we're about to discuss, you will be able to find some extra money to put toward your debts.

How much extra do you think you could come up with? Set an accelerator goal. On your *Monthly Cash Flow Plan*, add that amount to what you're currently paying on your lowest-balance debt and put the new total in the "Goal" column.

The Case Against 0 Percent Financing

Beware. Such "deals" often come with strings attached. In many cases, if you fail to finish paying for the item by the end of the promotional period, you will be socked for back interest.

For example, let's say you signed up for one year of 0 percent financing for a $2,000 bedroom set and then you miss the deadline on the final payment. The company may charge you 24 percent on the full amount. That will cost you another $480. And they'll likely throw in a late-payment fee to boot.[3]

Consider such a deal only when the following is true:

- You have researched the competition to see that the price they are offering at 0 percent financing really is the best deal around (often it is not—they're making up for the lost interest revenue by charging a higher price).
- You have the full amount of the price of the item in savings and will keep it in savings throughout the time that you are making payments (that way, you are not presuming you will have the money to make the payments—you actually have the money).
- You mark on your calendar when the payments are due, especially the last payment, so that you are sure to make your payments on time.

One note: Before accelerating the payoff of your debts, make sure you have at least one month's worth of essential living expenses in an emergency fund (your *If* savings account). Look at the *Monthly Cash Flow Plan* and total up all your absolutely essential expenses—those you would have to keep paying each month if you lost your job tomorrow, such as your mortgage or rent, utilities, food, and the like. That's how much you need in your *If* savings account before you start accelerating your debt payments. Put this money in a bank (traditional or online) or credit union savings or money market account.

Calculating Your Debt Freedom Date

It can be very motivating to figure out when you will be out of debt under different scenarios. To do so, go to www.crown.org and click on "Financial and Career Tools." Click on "Calculators" and then "Accelerated Debt Payoff Calculator." Follow the instructions, entering information from the "Debt Organizer" on page 23. On the calculator, the "Current Totals" row will tell you how long it will take to be out of debt if you fix your payments on today's minimum required payments. The "ADP Totals" row will tell you how much faster you'll be out of debt if you use the fix and roll approach. Then you can experiment with various accelerator amounts to see their impact.

Finding the Money to Accelerate Debt Repayment

There are three ways to find extra money to put toward your debts: selling possessions to raise money, increasing your income, or managing your spending more effectively. What follows are some ideas for each option. Some of the ideas will make sense and don't require a lot of effort; others will sound just plain crazy.

Here's why I'm including the crazy ones. Proverbs 3:27-28 states,

Do not withhold good from those who deserve it,
when it is in your power to act.
Do not say to your neighbor,
'Come back later; I'll give it tomorrow' —
when you now have it with you. (emphasis added)

The "when it is in your power to act" part stopped me in my tracks when I first read those verses. Whether something is in your power to act depends on your answer to the question "How serious are you about getting to a better place financially?" If you're serious, you'll consider even the crazy ideas, so keep an open mind as you read these ideas.

Selling Stuff

Take a good look around your house. Open the closets and cabinets. Have a look inside your garage. As you do, make a list of all the items you have not used in the last six to twelve months and put them up for sale. Hold a garage sale or sell your stuff on eBay (www.ebay.com) or Craigslist (www.craigslist.org). Let some friends know about the purpose of your sale and see if they'll contribute items, perhaps splitting the profits with you since you're managing the sale. Some may even donate items, letting you keep the full amount you make.

Increasing Income

If you're unemployed or underemployed (unable to pay all your bills on your income), pick up a part-time job. The average American adult watches more than two hours of television per day.[4] Transfer that time to a part-time job and you could earn a healthy amount of money that could be put toward your debts.

If increasing your income will help you get to a better place with your finances, set a goal for the amount and put it in the "Goal" column of your *Monthly Cash Flow Plan.*

Spending More Effectively

Within everyone's *Monthly Cash Flow Plan* are many opportunities to free up money. Here are some ways to do so. For any ideas you plan to implement, estimate the impact on the spending category that it pertains to, and enter new numbers in the "Goal" column of your *Monthly Cash Flow Plan.*

Housing. For most people, this is easily their largest expense. If you rent, consider moving to a less expensive apartment or house. When I started my first full-time job, I rented a beautiful two-story apartment and rented enough furniture to furnish every room. When my first bills came due, I was shocked to discover I was in way over my head. I was able to move to a studio apartment within the same complex, and I renegotiated the deal with the furniture company so that I was able to give back a lot of the furniture.

If you own your home, I recommend you spend no more than 25 percent of your monthly gross income on the combination of mortgage principal and interest, real estate taxes, and homeowners insurance. Any more than that and it's difficult to be generous and to save adequately. Of course, if your home is too expensive, moving won't be easy, but it's something you should consider.

That's what Hal and Dee did. When they were in their mid fifties, they found themselves with fifty thousand dollars of credit card and tax debt. That would have been bad enough, but they had been there before, which only made it worse. They had been riding a financial—not to mention emotional, spiritual, and marital—roller coaster for years.

Early in their marriage, they got behind on the payments for their first house. They had just become Christians, and Hal thought that somehow, some way God would swoop in and bail them out. They had faith but took no action. They lost that house to foreclosure.

Many years later, there they were again, right back in debt. Hal had been running a business that remodeled homes and built luxury spec homes. His last project didn't go well. Hal and Dee still had a strong faith, only this time they realized they needed to take some strong action as well.

Fueled by a commitment to pay back all of their debt and at the urging of some close friends, they closed Hal's business, sold their home, put most of their possessions in storage, and moved into a basement apartment in the home of some friends. The profit on their home allowed them to pay off much of their debt. Living virtually rent-free for three years enabled them to pay off the rest of their debt and save for a down payment on the townhouse where they now live.

None of that was easy. Hal had built his business from scratch, and shutting it down felt like a huge failure. Dee loved entertaining friends in their home. When they first thought of selling the house and moving into a small basement apartment, she felt as if she were losing part of who she was. But Hal and Dee agreed that closing Hal's business and selling their home were the right financial moves to make, and doing so brought some unexpected benefits. Hal says their financial stress had left them close to "throwing in the towel" on their marriage, but once they decided on their course of action, a weight lifted from their shoulders. Dee said, "I felt some of the same excitement as when we were newly married and lived in a one-bedroom apartment."

Shortly after shutting down his business, a friend from church asked Hal if he would be interested in becoming a financial advisor. Hal laughed at the idea, wondering how he could help others with their finances when his were in shambles. Over the next six years, Hal and Dee went from being fifty thousand dollars in debt to being completely out of debt. As for that crazy-sounding career move to begin managing other people's money? Today Hal has become such a respected financial advisor that he manages a fifty-million-dollar portfolio.

Hal says, "We don't know what lies ahead, but we know that God's hand is on us. We know we can trust him no matter what. Through this whole process—downsizing, redoing our lives—we can look back and see where God's hand was every step of the way. We can count on the fact that God loves us, his grace is sufficient, and his timing is perfect."

What about you? Is there anything you could do about your housing costs? Should you sell your house? Take in a renter? Keep asking yourself, *How serious am I?*

Maintenance/utilities. You probably already know the basics here, like managing your thermostat, not keeping your home too cool in the summer or too warm in the winter, and using compact fluorescent lightbulbs. But let's get more serious. Do you have a landline telephone *and* a cell phone? If so, how about dropping one? Do you have an Internet connection at home? This thought may make your jaw drop, but consider dropping the service. Internet service is one of many examples in which a want has become a perceived need for many of us. Is it really a need? Or is becoming debt-free more important? Besides, you can access the Internet for free at a public library and many coffee shops.

Transportation. One way to save on the cost of transportation is to raise your insurance deductibles. Just keep in mind that in doing so, you are, in essence, self-insuring for the amount of the deductible. Therefore, make sure you have the amount of the deductible in savings. Consider doing the same thing with your homeowners insurance.

Another cost-saving move is to drive less. Is public transportation an option? Could you walk or ride your bike to the grocery store? Are there any carsharing services where you live? This is relatively new concept (at least in the U.S.) in which companies will rent you a car on an hourly basis. See if your city offers a carsharing program at www. carsharing.net.

If you're a two-car family, consider becoming a one-car family. If you're a one-car family, think the unthinkable: becoming a no-car family.

Our family recently went from two vehicles to one. The car I was driving had 165,000 miles on it when a front spring broke, causing additional damage to the suspension. The cost of repairs was more than we were willing to pay, so we gave the car to a ministry that fixes cars and gives them to needy families. Because I work from home, it's easier for us to get by with one car than it might be for others. However, I'm discovering that many of the trips I used to take with the car were unnecessary. The money we're saving on gasoline, repairs, and insurance is coming in handy, as we recently had a third child.

Or you might consider whether commuting with a coworker is an option for you.

Income taxes. Getting a tax refund means you are overpaying on your taxes. I don't mind you getting a little bit back each year, say two hundred dollars. However, the average refund is more than two thousand dollars. If that's your situation, go to www.irs.gov, search for "Withholding Calculator," and calculate how much you should be paying in federal income taxes each year. Then contact your human resources department and ask to have withholding changed accordingly. Put the extra cash flow toward accelerated debt repayment.

A RAL Is Not Your Pal

Refund anticipation loans, or RALs, are extremely short-term loans. They last for the time between filing your return and receiving your refund, which usually amounts to just a few weeks. They're an extremely bad idea. If you ever walk through a retail store during tax season and see a table with a sign promoting "instant tax refunds," head down a different aisle. If you make the mistake of stopping to chat with the friendly folks manning the table, here's what you'll find out.

They'd be happy to prepare your tax return for you and write you a check for the amount of your refund, *minus* a tax preparation fee and a filing fee. There's nothing wrong with that, although you probably could have prepared and filed your own return.

Here's where things go south. *Your instant refund will also cost you fees that work out to hundreds of points of interest.*[5] RALs are close cousins of payday today loans. You want no part of either one.

Food. There are lots of ways to save on the cost of food. Shop with a list, use coupons, plan meals based on what's on sale, stock up on regularly used nonperishable items when they go on deep discount, and try some discount grocers. Certain stores have the best prices for items you buy regularly.

For example, most mornings I eat oatmeal for breakfast, which my wife, Jude, affectionately refers to as my horse food. Every time I shopped at our main grocery store, I'd visit the cereal aisle to see if the store brand of quick oats was on sale. Whenever it went on sale, I would stock up. But then it seemed as though it were never on sale, so I checked a nearby discount grocer (Aldi) and found that its everyday price was cheaper than the sale price of the store brand at the other grocery store. Now I trot over to Aldi whenever I need more oats.

Clothing. The next time you feel the *need* to buy clothing, rummage through your closet. Find something you haven't worn in a long time and try it on. It may still look good on you. Many of us have clothes we hardly ever wear. Once a month, hold a back-of-the-closet day and see if you can come up with something suitable to wear that you haven't worn in a while. You may find that you don't *need* to buy clothing nearly as often.

Gifts. If you're having a tough time meeting your monthly expenses, the last thing you need to spend money on right now is gifts. Spend some time with friends on their birthdays instead of spending money. Is there a project they could use some help with? They'll welcome your assistance and, more important, be grateful for your company. Time is far more valuable than anything you can buy at the store.

Or make a simple homemade meal for someone. It will be less expensive than a store-bought gift, and people will likely appreciate it more because of the time you spent making it for them. Some friends of mine buy nice but inexpensive pie plates and then make pies for their friends during the holidays. The recipients get a homemade treat and a reusable pie plate that brings back memories of the thoughtful gift.

Entertainment. Make it a game to find as many free or inexpensive fun things to do near where you live. There are probably some great parks you've never visited, free days at museums, and, of course, free stuff at the library, sometimes including museum and zoo passes and more. When I was digging myself into debt, I used to play golf at a course near Chicago where they hold a PGA Tour event. It was not cheap. As part of my debt-recovery process, I opened my eyes a bit wider and discovered some good park district courses that charge a fraction of what the other course charges. Chicago even has two affordable park district courses with some holes bordering Lake Michigan.

You can also save on the cost of entertainment by cutting the cable. With fewer stations to choose from, you'll probably watch less television overall, which has been proven to be good for people's finances. Research has shown that the more television you watch, the more you spend.[6] In part, that's due to the many commercials on television. It's also because the characters in many shows live more expensive lifestyles than the average person, and that encourages viewers to try to emulate those lifestyles.

Health. Stress goes hand in hand with poor health habits. When we're under pressure, we tend to overdo the sweets and underdo the exercise. Of course, during tough times, we need exercise and healthy food more than ever. So, for the sake of your sanity, get out for a walk, go for a bike ride, or take a run. You don't need an expensive health-club membership for any of that. Focus on foods that are good for you. If your accountability partners happen to be exercisers and healthy eaters, ask them for some support in these areas, too. If not, find someone else to be your accountability and encouragement partner for these things. Practicing healthy habits will be good for your mood, and you just might save on medical bills as well.

Professional services. For families with children, babysitting costs can really add up. Find a family with whom you can trade babysitting duties.

Turning It Up One More Notch

Here's one more idea for freeing up money that you can put toward your debt. It is perhaps the craziest idea yet and probably the one that will have the greatest impact in the shortest amount of time. Go on a spending fast.

Julie has gone on several spending fasts over the years. Her most recent one lasted six months. Of course, she didn't stop spending completely; she just didn't spend on anything that seemed discretionary. That meant no new clothing, shoes, jewelry, towels, pillows, movies, CDs, hair products other than essentials, or restaurant meals that were not work related. Applying the "no discretionary spending" rule to her grocery shopping, she whittled her shopping list down to twelve essential items. She kept her cell phone but took it down to the least expensive plan, which was ten bucks a month.

At first she felt deprived. Gifts were the hardest thing to give up. She said, "I love to give gifts, and I'm big on hospitality. Clothing was tough too, but I learned to get creative and put together new combinations of clothing."

It wasn't debt that motivated Julie to go on the fast; it was a desire to give more money away. And it worked. The fast enabled her to give away nearly 50 percent of her income, whereas she used to give away around 20 percent.

When her fast ended, she no longer felt deprived. In fact, she found it difficult to spend money. To celebrate the end of her fast, some friends took her—where else?—shopping! At midnight they went to a discount retailer that's open twenty-four hours. Even though the store had thousands of items to choose from, Julie left there with just a new skirt and a pair of socks. Although Julie has gone back to spending money on gifts, many of her spending habits have been forever altered. She now gives away about 30 percent of her income.

She says that the fast helped her see with new eyes the influence of our culture. "I had allowed my sense of normal to be shaped by the behavior of people around me. People think they don't have any margin, but it's because their 'normal' is so out of whack, from the food we consume to the clothes we wear to our choices of entertainment to the frequency with which we buy shoes or pillows or winter coats. Who said that we need new stuff every year?"

Note: For more ideas on spending effectively, go to www.money purposejoy.com and sign up for my free e-newsletter, "Matt About Money." Twice a month, I share the best new ideas I've come across.

Added Help

In addition to having an accountability partner, you may also find it helpful to meet with someone trained to help you develop a workable *Monthly Cash Flow Plan*. Here are four places to look:

1. Good $ense. This is a national ministry that I have been involved with for many years. Founded at Willow Creek Community Church in suburban Chicago in the late 1980s, this ministry is now offered at a couple thousand churches nationwide, many of which provide free confidential budget counseling. If your church has a Good $ense ministry with budget counselors, set up a meeting with one of them.

2. Crown. This is another excellent national financial ministry, with trained Money Map Coaches in many parts of the country who are available for free budget counseling. Go to www.crown.org, click on "In My Area," and then "Find a Coach Now." Crown also offers budget counseling online and over the phone.

3. Consumer-credit counseling. These offices are known for their debt management plans, but they also offer budget counseling. Sessions range in price from free to twenty dollars. Go to the National Foundation for Credit Counseling website at www.DebtAdvice.org, click on "Take the First Step," and then "Member Agency Locator."

4. Employee assistance programs. If you work for a large company, you may have access to an Employee Assistance Program. Call your human resources department to find out. These confidential programs often offer financial counseling and referral programs.

What About You?

Okay, you've heard some radical ideas: Sell your home, take a part-time job, go on a spending fast. Which options are "in your power to act"? Write down the action steps you will take.

_____

_____

_____

_____

_____

By now the "Goal" columns of your *Monthly Cash Flow Plan* should be complete. Take those numbers and enter them in the "Goals" row at the top of your *Monthly Cash Flow Tracker*. Use these goals to guide your spending in each expense category.

Next, we'll look at strategies for paying back specific types of debts.

WRITE IT ON YOUR HEART

Commit to the LORD whatever you do, and your plans will succeed. (Proverbs 16:3)

Chapter 4

"Unsecured" Debt Solutions

Creditors have better memories than debtors.

— BENJAMIN FRANKLIN

Accoording to a famous poem, "a rose is a rose is a rose." Not so with debt. There are many types of debt, each with its own ramifications for falling behind on the payments, and each with its own unique solutions. *Unsecured* debt, meaning debts for which there is no collateral, include credit card, medical, tax, and education debt.

The first thing you need to know about unsecured debt is that just because there is no collateral behind the debt doesn't mean the creditor can't create some collateral. If you fall behind on your payments, the creditor can place a lien on your property, go after money in your bank accounts, and force some of your income to be sent its way each month via wage garnishment. So if you're having trouble making payments on unsecured debt, don't let your problems linger. Take action.

Credit Card Debt

If you tried the steps in the previous chapter and still can't make even the minimum payments on your debts, get in touch with a local credit-counseling agency. Among other services, these agencies offer debt management plans (DMP), in which they negotiate with your creditors on your behalf, usually lowering the monthly payments and often stopping additional late and over-limit fees. You will send the credit-counseling agency one check each month, which the office will divvy up among your creditors. When you begin working with a credit-counseling office, many collection activities will stop.

Credit-counseling offices are funded, in part, by the credit card companies, which make "fair share" contributions to the credit-counseling agencies based on a percentage of the amounts the agencies collect on their behalf. Because of this relationship, credit-counseling agencies are able to work out reasonable payment plans with your creditors.

There are thousands of such offices around the country. Be careful in choosing one, as a number of unscrupulous players have entered the field. Find a local office associated with the National Foundation for Credit Counseling (NFCC). Founded in 1951, the NFCC is the oldest and largest network of community-based, nonprofit credit-counseling agencies in the nation. All NFCC counselors are certified credit counselors, and all of the agencies are accredited by an independent third party. You can search for an office near you on the NFCC website at www.DebtAdvice.org or by calling 800-388-2227. Once you find a local office accredited by the NFCC, go a step further and check with the Better Business Bureau via its website (www.bbb.org) to see if any unresolved complaints have been filed against the office. If you can't find a credit-counseling office near you or prefer not to visit the office in person, check for one that offers its services online or over the phone.

Once you select an office, get all fee information up front and in writing. Typical debt management plan fees include a one-time set-up fee of about fifty dollars and monthly fees of thirty-five dollars. If your finances are really tight, you may be eligible to work with an agency at no cost because one of the NFCC's standards for membership is a willingness to work with people regardless of their ability to pay.

One sign that you're talking with the wrong agency is if they require much higher fees. Another warning sign is if the agency tries to put you into a DMP without first looking for other solutions to your situation, such as helping you find ways to lower your expenses or increase your income. According to Gail Cunningham, spokesperson for the NFCC, "If we've pared the budget, explored income options, and there still isn't enough money to service living expenses and debt obligations, then we'll consider a DMP as one of the resolution options."[1]

A debt management plan can be used with only certain unsecured debts, such as credit card and medical debt. Student loans cannot be renegotiated through credit-counseling offices. Whether tax debt can go through a DMP depends on where you live. At the least, a credit-counseling office can provide guidance about tax debt. You will have to keep making your mortgage and vehicle payments separately. However, the NFCC also has a large number of certified housing counselors who can help you with foreclosure-prevention assistance.

Although working with a credit-counseling office should not hurt your credit score, it may impact your credit report. If one of your creditors reports that you are on a DMP, it could hinder your ability to get credit.

Opt for a Debt Management Plan, Not a Debt Settlement Plan

A debt settlement plan, sometimes referred to as a debt elimination program, sounds similar to a debt management plan, but there is a world of difference. A debt management plan will lower your monthly payments, whereas debt settlement companies purport to lower your balances.

Such companies often advise people to stop making payments to their creditors and to send them the payments instead. The companies say they will save the money until they have enough to make a settlement offer. But there's no guarantee that a creditor will accept such an offer. Plus, when you stop paying your debts, your balances can grow quickly because the interest and fees continue. In addition, your credit score will likely take a hit. All those missed payments might prompt creditors to garnish your wages and place liens on your property. Further, if the debt is settled, you may have to pay taxes on the portion of the debt that was forgiven. My advice? Do not work with debt settlement companies.

Medical Debt

You don't have to be uninsured to struggle with medical bills. An estimated 79 million Americans are finding it difficult to pay their medical bills, and more than 60 percent of these people have insurance.[2] If you have medical bills you can't afford, get in touch with the medical provider's office as soon as possible. Unpaid bills might get turned over to a bill collector, which will hurt your credit score. You could also be sued, which could lead to your wages being garnished.

If medical bills are a problem for you, here are some options.

Ask for a Plan.

Call your medical provider's financial aid office and see about being put on a payment plan in which you pay off your debt over time. The debt may not be reported to the credit bureaus, and medical facilities typically don't charge interest. Such plans usually need to be completed in twelve to twenty-four months but may be allowed to run longer.

According to Gail Cunningham, of the NFCC, credit counselors could help you negotiate a workable plan with your medical provider, sometimes reducing debt balances or even getting debts written off.[3]

Ask for a Discount.

At many medical facilities, free or discounted care is available to patients based on how their income stacks up against federal poverty guidelines. Some offer discounted or free care for patients who don't have insurance, patients with insurance but who can't afford their co-pay amounts, and patients with insurance who incur charges their insurance won't cover. Keep in mind that you can't always count on medical providers to bring this to your attention.

When Tim's young son started stuttering, his pediatrician suggested having the child evaluated by a speech therapist at the hospital with which the pediatrician was affiliated. After talking with the young boy for thirty minutes, the therapist told Tim that the child did not need speech therapy. When Tim got a bill for five hundred dollars a few weeks later, he was stunned. It was bad enough that his insurance provider denied coverage, but the amount seemed exorbitant. There had been no diagnostic tests performed, and the therapist spent just half an hour talking with the boy. When Tim called the billing office to complain, he didn't mention that his insurance refused to cover the cost; he was trying to fight what he thought was an inflated charge. The hospital stood firm. When Tim finally mentioned that his insurance would not cover the cost, a billing department representative matter-of-factly reduced the bill by 40 percent. That was the hospital's policy.

Later, Tim discovered that his town's school system offered free speech screening and, if needed, free speech therapy. The lesson for all of us? Be proactive in checking your medical provider's policies about discounted or free care by asking your physician, calling the medical facility's financial aid office, or looking on the facility's website. Also, see if your community or school system provides free screenings or treatment.

If you do not have health insurance, here are a couple of other resources to explore:

- The Association of American Medical Colleges lists community-based medical programs for the uninsured here: www.aamc .org/uninsured/start.htm.
- Many states offer free or low-cost insurance for kids. To search for a program in your state, go to www.insurekidsnow.gov /states.asp.
- Many independent nonprofit organizations provide financial assistance to patients suffering from specific diseases, such as cancer. The Patient Advocate Foundation (www.patientadvo cate.org) provides links to such charities.

Beware of Medical Financing Plans

Doctors', dentists', and even veterinarians' offices are the newest marketing venues for credit cards, installment loans, and other forms of financing.

Medical credit cards differ from other credit cards in that they are accepted at only participating medical providers. Lenders are promoting such cards as a way for doctors to make more money and get paid more promptly and as a way for patients to get the treatments they need or want immediately. A promotion for Capital One Healthcare Finance says, "Procedures like liposuction, hair restoration, tummy tucks, and more are now within reach."[4]

Consumer Reports warns that medical credit cards and other financing plans offered by medical providers often carry exorbitant interest rates, and by agreeing to a finance plan, some patients are losing their ability to bargain for lower prices or obtain charity care. Some patients have even reported feeling pressured to finance their medical care while sedated or recovering from treatment.[5] Plus, credit cards and other medical financing plans charge interest, whereas a repayment plan worked out through your medical provider's financial aid office typically does not charge interest. So before signing up for a medical credit card or other form of financing through your medical provider, contact the provider's financial aid office to check on the availability of discounts or a no-interest repayment plan.

Look for Billing Errors.

Pat Palmer, founder and president of Medical Billing Advocates of America, estimates that of the many medical bills she has reviewed over the past fifteen years, 80 percent contain errors.[6] Among the common billing problems are duplicate billing of services under different descriptions; the use of incorrect symptom, diagnosis, or procedure codes; services that were not provided; overly marked-up procedures and supplies; and plain old mistakes.

I can vouch for this. We recently received a receipt from a medical provider involved in the delivery of our third child. I had submitted payment over the phone, so I expected the receipt but not the amount. A couple of zeros were inadvertently added to a $180 bill, causing

$18,000 to be added to our credit card. By the time I called about it, the provider had already corrected the mistake, but it made me wonder how often smaller mistakes slip by.

Palmer recommends asking for detailed statements instead of the summary statements many medical providers usually send. By reviewing a detailed statement, you may be able to catch some errors. Maybe there's a charge for a medication that you know isn't correct because you're allergic to that medication. Perhaps there's a charge for more time in a recovery room than you actually spent. But there may be some mistakes you cannot detect. That's why you might consider the use of someone trained to detect billing errors, such as a medical advocate.

Enlist the Help of a Medical Advocate.

For an hourly fee or a percentage of the cost savings, medical advocates review bills for errors and help people get reimbursed. Palmer's Medical Billing Advocates of America has a website with links to advocates around the country at www.billadvocates.com.

Also, check to see if your employer offers access to medical advocates. Thousands of companies have added health-advocate services to their benefits. The services, ranging from helping with medical billing disputes to providing information about certain health conditions and treatment options, are often free to employees.

Get Help for the Cost of Prescription Drugs.

When Eric underwent a kidney transplant, his employer-provided health insurance covered only a portion of the $250,000 procedure, so he was happy to discover that Medicare provides extensive coverage for end-stage renal failure even among people younger than sixty-five. The government agency is also covering most of the cost of his expensive monthly medication regimen for three years. But Eric, who is thirty-three, will need to take the medicine for the rest of his life, so how will he manage the expense once Medicare's coverage ends?

There are a number of organizations that provide help for people who can't afford their medications. Check out the following to see if you qualify:

- NeedyMeds (www.needymeds.org) helps patients find local assistance programs.
- Partnership for Prescription Assistance (www.pparx.org) helps patients search for assistance among nearly five hundred assistance programs.
- RxAssist (www.RxAssist.org) helps patients search for assistance for medication.
- Together Rx Access (www.togetherrxaccess.com) offers discounts on the retail prices of hundreds of drugs.
- Merck (www.merckhelps.com) and Pfizer (www.pfizerhelpful answers.com) offer discount cards for many of their medications.
- Rx Outreach (www.rxoutreach.com) and Xubex Pharmaceutical Services (www.xubex.com) offer discounts on hundreds of generic medications.
- Walmart, Target, Safeway, and other retail chains offer many generic drugs at low costs.[7]

Tax Debt

Knowing that you're likely to face a big tax bill may tempt you not to file your tax return, but that will only leave you with more expense in the form of a penalty for not filing. So file your return, paying as much as you can.

Next, you'll have to figure out how to pay the rest of what you owe. If you don't pay your income taxes, the IRS may garnish your wages or place a lien on your property. Instead of letting things get that out of control, get in touch with the IRS as soon as possible and explore the following options.

Installment Agreement

If you owe the IRS money, you may be eligible to pay off what you owe, plus interest and penalties, in monthly installments. You'll have to pay a fee of about a hundred dollars to establish an installment agreement, or half of that amount if you agree to have your payments automatically deducted from your bank account. To learn more, go to www.irs.gov. Under "I need to . . ." choose "Set Up a Payment Plan."

Temporary Delay

If the IRS determines you can't pay any of your tax debt, collection may be delayed until your financial condition improves. However, your debt will grow because penalties and interest will be charged until you pay the full amount. During the temporary delay, the IRS will continue to review your ability to pay and may file a tax lien.

Offer in Compromise

If you cannot afford an installment agreement, you can make an "offer in compromise," in which you offer to settle your tax debt in one lump sum totaling less than what you actually owe. However, the IRS has been accepting fewer and fewer of such offers. Plus, it's a time-consuming process, there is an application fee, and most applicants have to make an upfront, nonrefundable partial payment when they apply, so make sure you feel confident about meeting the requirements. You'll need to demonstrate that your financial distress is such that you will never be able to pay back everything you owe.

Additional Help

If you are having a difficult time resolving an IRS tax dispute, contact the IRS Taxpayer Advocate Service. This is an independent organization within the IRS designed to help taxpayers experiencing significant hardships. To get in touch, call 1-877-777-4778.

You can learn more about all of these options at www.irs.gov (see IRS Publication 594).

Avoid Outside Tax-Assistance Companies

You may be tempted to turn to a private company for help in settling your tax debt, but beware. There are often steep upfront fees involved and some unscrupulous players out there. In fact, the nation's largest tax-resolution company recently settled with eighteen states over allegations that it misled consumers and failed to produce results.[8]

Student Loans

If you are having a tough time making your student loan payments, call the company that services your loan and discuss the following options.

Loan consolidation. If you have multiple federal student loans, you may be able to consolidate them into one loan at a lower interest rate. You may even "consolidate" one loan into a new loan in order to obtain a better interest rate. The rates change on July 1 each year.

Only a handful of lenders offer private student loan consolidation, and those that do have made their standards more stringent. You'll probably have to go through the U.S. Department of Education's Federal Direct Loan Program. To learn more, estimate payments with an online calculator, and apply, go to www.loanconsolidation.ed.gov.

An alternative repayment plan. When you first agreed to your student loan, it was probably for a ten-year term. However, you can change repayment plans as long as the plan you switch into has a longer payoff term than your current loan. Switching to a plan with a longer payoff period will reduce your monthly payments. Of course, if you take the full amount of time to pay off the loan, you'll end up paying more in interest. However, all federal student loans allow for prepayment without penalty, so you could always pay more than the required amount in order to accelerate the payoff. Just be sure to include with any added payment a note stating that it is to be applied to the principal balance.

There are also plans designed around your income. If you have a federal loan and your income is low, you may be eligible for an income-based repayment (IBR) plan. Under such a plan, your payments can stretch for as long as twenty-five years, at which point the government will cancel any remaining balance. The catch is that income taxes will be due on the canceled amount.

Deferment. If you are having financial problems but are not in default on your student loan, you can request a deferment of up to three years. If you have a federally subsidized loan, the government will even pay the interest while the loan is in deferment. You still have to pay back the loan, but you can put your payments on hold for a while. You may qualify for a deferment if you are unemployed, facing some other economic hardship, serving in the military or National Guard (if you are on active duty, you may qualify for a deferment longer than three years), or have chosen to go to school at least half time. To see all of the circumstances that may make you eligible for a deferment or forbearance, go to the Department of Education Federal Student Aid website at www.dlssonline.com and click on "Forms."

Forbearance. If you don't qualify for a deferment, you can ask for forbearance, which is a temporary reduction or postponement of payments for up to three years. Interest always accrues on forbearance and will be added to your loan balance once you start repaying again.

Loan forgiveness. You may be eligible to have some of your student loan erased if you take part in a program such as the Peace Corps (www.peacecorps.gov), Americorps (www.americorps.org), or Teach For America (www.teachforamerica.org). There is also a relatively new Loan Forgiveness for Public Service Employees Program, which provides federal student loan forgiveness for many public service employees. You have to have made at least ten years' worth of payments under certain repayment plans beginning October 1, 2007.

Student loan forgiveness is also available should you become totally and permanently disabled.

For more information about student loan repayment and forgiveness options, go to:

- www.studentaid.ed.gov (click on "Repaying Your Loans")
- www.finaid.org (click on "Loans")

Rehabilitating a defaulted loan. Although student loan debt is not secured debt (your lender can't take your car or home if you don't keep up with the payments), the government can garnish your wages, intercept tax refunds, charge you hefty collection fees, and sue you. There is no statute of limitations for the collection of defaulted student loans.

If your loan is already in default, get in touch with the company that services your loan to discuss the options for rehabilitating your loan. The details vary by the type of loan you have, but all methods for loan rehabilitation involve making voluntary (as opposed to payments via wage garnishment) on-time payments for a certain number of months.

If you've contacted the company that services your loan and have a dispute you cannot resolve, contact the Federal Student Aid ombudsman's office at www.ombudsman.ed.gov or call 877-557-2575.

Dealing with Debt Collectors

If you're getting calls from bill collectors, here's what you need to know.

If they are third-party debt collectors (as opposed to your original creditors), you can ask them to stop contacting you and they must adhere to that request. Your original creditors are under no such obligation. But it's usually a good idea to work with debt collectors because getting them to stop contacting you does not protect you from being sued, and you don't want that.

By law, debt collectors may contact you in person, by mail, telephone, telegram, or fax. However, they may not contact you before 8:00 a.m. or after 9:00 p.m. They may contact other people in regard to your debt but only to find out where you live, what your phone number is, or where you work. They may not, in most cases, communicate with anyone about your debt other than you, your attorney, a credit reporting agency, or the original creditor. Debt collectors may not threaten to harm or imprison you, use profane language, use false or misleading statements, or use deception to make you accept a collect call or pay for a telegram.

If you'd rather not deal with a third-party bill collector, contact the collections department of your original creditor and see if they will work with you directly. You'll probably be asked to negotiate with the collections agency initially, work out a repayment plan, and make a few payments under the plan. At that point, the original creditor may be willing to work with you again directly.[9]

Remember that debt collectors are not your friends. Treat them cordially, but make the conversations strictly business. Tell them what you can and cannot do about your debt.

If a bill collector offers to settle the debt for less than what you owe, there may be income taxes due on the forgiven amount. If the amount forgiven is six hundred dollars or more, you'll probably receive tax form 1099-C at the end of the year.

For more information about what debt collectors may and may not do, go to www.ftc.gov, click on "Consumer Protection," then "Consumer Information," then "Credit & Loans," then "In Debt?" and then "Fair Debt Collection." If you have any problems with a debt collector, contact your state's attorney general's office. You can also file a complaint through the Federal Trade Commission's website at www.ftccomplaintassistant.gov.[10]

Should You Help Someone Obtain a Loan?

In Proverbs 22:26, we are warned, "Don't agree to guarantee another person's debt or put up security for someone else" (NLT). (Also see Proverbs 6:1-5; 11:15; 17:18). When you cosign for a loan, you are assuming complete responsibility for that debt if the borrower defaults. If you cosign for a loan for someone who ends up filing for bankruptcy, that person may be protected from attempts to collect on the loan, but you will not be protected.

Bottom line? Don't cosign for someone else's loan. This even goes for family members. Having to make good on a loan that a family member can't afford can harm your relationship with that person. If you really want to help a family member with a purchase, consider giving the person the money with no expectation of repayment.

Now that we've explored the options for repaying various types of unsecured debts, let's take a look at secured debts.

WRITE IT ON YOUR HEART

I can do all things through Christ who strengthens me.
(Philippians 4:13, NKJV)

Chapter 5

"Secured" Debt Solutions

A man builds a fine house, and now he has a master, and
a task for life.

— RALPH WALDO EMERSON

Secured debt is collateralized debt. That means there's an asset securing the loan you used to "buy" the item. If you stop making payments on that item, the lender can take it back. The two most common
types of secured debts are home and vehicle debts. Alimony and child
support debts are secured too—secured with your freedom. If you fall
behind on these payments, you could land in jail.

Mortgage Debt

Missing even one payment on your home can begin a fast downward
spiral toward losing your home. First your credit score will take a hit.
Then you'll start getting unpleasant letters from your lender reminding
you that your payment is late and imposing a fee. After sixty to ninety
days of no payments, your lender will usually write again, this time
stating that your loan is in default. Translation: Bring your loan current, including back payments plus late and legal fees, or the foreclosure
process will begin. Your lender may also accelerate your loan, meaning
the full loan balance becomes due. Unless you have a big pile of cash in

the bank, the only way to come up with the money will be by refinancing your home, which will be more difficult at this point because of the hits your credit score has taken from those missed mortgage payments. If you don't pay your mortgage in full, typically your home will be put up for foreclosure sale.

Two added bits of pain are associated with foreclosure. First, after your home is sold, you may still owe money to the lender. That could happen if there's a difference between what you owe and what the lender received at the sale. In some states, the lender is entitled to the deficiency. The lender may turn this over to a collection agency or could sue you for the amount. Second, foreclosure will stay on your credit record for seven to ten years. Clearly, you don't want any of this to happen.

Options for Keeping Your Home

These include:

Traditional refinancing. If your mortgage payments are putting a strain on your finances, possibly because you have an adjustable-rate mortgage and your rate has increased, assess whether you could afford your home under somewhat better terms, such as a lower interest rate. As I said earlier, my rule of thumb is to devote no more than 25 percent of your monthly gross income to the combination of your mortgage principal and interest, property taxes, and insurance. If the amount is much higher than that and you'd like to stay in your home, compare your interest rate with current rates (check rates at www.bankrate.com). If today's rates are better than what you're paying, use the "refinance" calculator in the "mortgate" tab on the same site to see if a lower rate will bring your monthly housing costs down closer to that 25 percent benchmark.

If so, if you have equity in your home and you are current on your payments, consider applying for a new loan.

Foreclosure prevention refinancing. If it looks as though you may miss a payment on your mortgage or if you've already missed some payments, get in touch with your lender as soon as possible. Amazingly, more than half of people who lose their homes through foreclosure never even bother to talk with their lender.[1] Contacting your lender signals that you want to keep your home and you'll be sent what's known as a workout package. You'll need to fill out this packet of financial forms and return it to the lender for an assessment of what options may be viable for you (see the next section).

A good next step is to get in touch with a trained housing counselor. Such counselors are available at no cost through several nonprofit organizations. There are plenty of for-profit foreclosure-prevention companies that would love your business, but there's no need to go that route when excellent free help is available.

The U.S. Department of Housing and Urban Development (HUD) maintains a list of approved housing-counseling organizations on its website at www.hud.gov/foreclosure. The following are two other organizations that offer information to struggling homeowners on their websites and referrals to HUD-approved housing counselors:

- The Homeownership Preservation Foundation (www.995hope .org, 1-888-995-HOPE) is a member of the Hope Now Alliance, an alliance between HUD-approved counseling agents, servicers, investors, and other mortgage market participants. It offers guidance online and over the phone.
- The National Foundation for Credit Counseling (www. HousingHelpNow.org, 1-866-845-2227) offers guidance over the phone or in person through a national network of accredited credit-counseling agencies.

Foreclosure laws vary by state (you can see your state's foreclosure laws at www.foreclosurelaw.org), but a foreclosure counselor will help you better understand the following options and suggest which one may work best for you.

Loan modification. Your lender may agree to make a permanent change to the terms of your contract in order to make your payments more feasible. Modifications may include lowering your interest rate, changing it from a variable rate to a fixed rate, extending the term of the loan, reducing the loan balance, or folding missed payments and fees into future payments.

If you are offered a modification, be cautious. One study of homeowners whose mortgages were modified in early 2008 found that over half had fallen behind on their payments within six months.[2] Especially problematic were modifications that added missed payments to future payments, thereby increasing the homeowners' monthly payments. Modifications that work better are those that reduce the loan balance.

"Hope for Homeowners." This is a specific FHA loan modification program for homeowners who are at risk of default, already in default, or even in certain stages of foreclosure. Under the program, your mortgage could be refinanced for between 90 and 96.5 percent of its current value. If your home has gone down in value, your lender is essentially writing down your current mortgage to that new lower value. Loan terms may also be extended from thirty years to forty years, which will further reduce your monthly payment. To be eligible:

- Your home needs to be your primary residence and you must have no ownership interest in any other residential property.
- Your mortgage must have originated on or before January 1, 2008, and you must have made at least six payments.
- You must not have been convicted of fraud in the past ten years, intentionally defaulted on debts, or knowingly or willingly provide material false information to obtain your existing mortgage.

Note that the program is voluntary. Lenders are not forced to participate, and they'll want to explore all other options first.

Another important provision involves equity sharing. You will be required to share with the FHA any equity created at the beginning of the new mortgage as well as a portion of any future appreciation. For example, let's say you have a $300,000 mortgage on a house that is now valued at just $200,000. If a lender agrees to the Hope for Homeowners program (remember, it's voluntary) and provides a $180,000 mortgage (90 percent of the new appraised value) in the first year of the new loan, FHA will own all of the $20,000 of equity created by the new mortgage. That percentage decreases gradually to 50 percent after five years. FHA will also own a portion of all equity created through the home's future appreciation.

This program runs through the end of September 2011. For more information, see www.hud.gov and www.fha.gov.

Forbearance. Under this option, your lender agrees to temporarily allow you to pay less than the amount due each month or to even suspend your payments for a period of time. At the end of that time, you resume making payments along with either a lump sum or additional partial payments until the missed payments are brought current. This may be an option if your income is temporarily reduced, perhaps through short-term disability or a period of unemployment, and you expect to resume working again in the near future. However, a lender will be more likely to agree to a forbearance once you're working again because this gives the lender more confidence that you'll be able to make up the missed payments.

Reorganization bankruptcy. One final option for keeping your home is to file for a Chapter 13 bankruptcy. Doing so will stop a foreclosure preceding, allowing you to keep your home by making up missed payments over the course of a three-to-five-year repayment plan. Of course, your income must be sufficient for making the current mortgage payments in addition to the missed payments. (I'll say more about bankruptcy in chapter 8.)

Property Taxes

Getting behind on your property taxes could result in the loss of your home, just as getting behind on your mortgage payments could. If you are having difficulty coming up with your property tax payment, get in touch with your county's taxing authority. (In Chicago, for example, that's the Cook County Treasurer's Office.) It may be able to offer you a payment plan. If you don't pay your property taxes, your home may be sold in a tax sale.

Options for Giving Up Your Home

It may be that your home is just too expensive for you and you would be better off living somewhere else. Here are some options to consider:

Selling your home. If you have equity in your home and could sell it for enough to be able to pay off the loan, this is the best way to get out of an unaffordable home. Of course, it may not be that simple.

Short sale. If you can no longer afford the payments on your home and its value has gone down below what you paid for it, your lender may agree to a short sale. By doing so, your lender is agreeing to accept less than your mortgage amount and forgive the rest. You will list your home for sale at its current appraised price and be allowed to continue to live there while no longer having to make payments. It's important to keep the house in good condition to help with the sales process. If it does not sell, you will likely face foreclosure.

Deed in lieu of foreclosure. Under this scenario, you transfer the property title to the lender in exchange for cancellation of your debt. You will give up any equity in the property. During periods of heavy foreclosure activity, most lenders will be hesitant to agree to a deed in lieu of foreclosure. They would rather have you try to sell the house than take responsibility for doing so themselves.

A short sale or deed in lieu of foreclosure may sound appealing, but be aware that your lender will report either one to the credit bureaus in a manner that is just as damaging to your credit score as a foreclosure, according to Barry Paperno, Consumer Operations Manager for Fair Isaac.[3]

For more information about avoiding foreclosure, the Mortgage Bankers Association offers guidance at www.homeloanlearningcenter .com.

Preparing for the Loss of Your Home

If it's inevitable that you will lose your home through foreclosure, a short sale, or a deed in lieu of foreclosure, it is likely that you will be able to stay in the house for several months without making any payments. How you handle your finances during that time is important.

According to Michele Johnson, CEO of Consumer Credit Counseling Service in Las Vegas, individuals should use the time to shore up their finances: "The person losing their home will likely have to rent an apartment next, and with a foreclosure on their record, they will have to come up with a sizeable deposit. So, during this window of time, when they don't have a mortgage payment, they should focus on building savings and paying down other debts."[4]

Taxes on Forgiven Mortgage Debt

It used to be that debt forgiven by a lender was taxed as income. However, the Mortgage Forgiveness Debt Relief Act of 2007 allows people to exclude certain principle residence debt forgiven in 2007, 2008, and 2009.

You will still have to report the forgiven debt on Form 982. On the IRS website (www.irs.gov), search for "Mortgage Forgiveness Debt Relief Act" to check whether mortgage debt that you have had forgiven qualifies for exclusion from being taxed.

A Note for Renters

If you rent your home and are having a tough time affording the cost, talk to your landlord. You may be able to negotiate a lower rent payment, move to a less expensive place owned by the landlord, or do maintenance work in exchange for part or all of your rent. Be sure to put the new agreement in writing and get the landlord to sign the agreement.

Vehicle Debt

If you're struggling with a car payment, call your lender as soon as possible; otherwise, your car may be repossessed. Whereas foreclosure can take many months, car repossession can happen much more quickly, sometimes after just one missed payment.

Ways to Avoid Repossession of Your Car

Here are some options if you're struggling with your car payment:

Refinance. If interest rates on vehicle loans have dropped (check www.bankrate.com), look into refinancing your vehicle. To qualify for refinancing, your car may need to be less than five years old and you may need to still owe at least $7,500. Of course, your car also needs to be worth more than what you owe, which is not always the case. You can get an estimate of its current value from Kelley Blue Book at www .kbb.com. When shopping for a loan, credit unions often offer the best rates.

Loan modification. Your lender may agree to rewrite your vehicle loan in a way that reduces your monthly payments. This typically involves a longer-term loan, which, of course, means you will be in debt longer and pay more in interest over the life of your loan.

An extension. Under this scenario, a missed payment is added to the end of your loan period. Most lenders will grant one extension per year and may charge a fee. Look into this option if your inability to make the payments appears to be temporary. Usually an extension is granted only if you are current on your payments.

If Your Car Is Repossessed . . .

If the amount you owe on a vehicle is less than the finance company gets when selling your car after repossessing it, you may owe the deficiency plus the costs for repossessing, storing, and selling the car. However, about half of all states do not impose deficiency balances on personal property if you paid relatively little (one thousand to four thousand in most cases) for the property in the first place. If you own few assets, the lender may forgive the deficiency as well, but you will likely owe taxes on the amount that was forgiven.

One way to minimize the deficiency is to ask for a contract reinstatement, in which you get the car back by making up any missed payments and fees. That will enable you to sell it yourself. You may not get the full amount that you owe on the vehicle (then again, you might), but you'll probably get more than the lender will get in a repossession sale, leaving you owing less of a deficiency.

Leased Vehicles

If you are leasing a vehicle and are having a tough time with the payments, getting out of the lease can be expensive. Check the terms in your contract. There will probably be an early-termination fee; however, this may be negotiable. You also may be able to extend the terms, resulting in a lower monthly payment.

A more appealing option is what's known as a lease assumption or transfer, in which someone else takes over your lease. Websites such as www.leasetrader.com and www.swapalease.com facilitate assumptions. Check with your leasing company to see if it allows lease transfers; many do. Usually there will be a fee for transferring your lease to someone else, but it will typically be less than an early termination fee. Of course, the person taking over your lease has to qualify with your financing company through a credit check and other steps you had to take when you signed for the original lease.[5]

Alimony and Child Support

If you fall behind on alimony or child support payments, you could be sued or have your wages garnished, your tax refund intercepted, or a lien placed against your property. You could even end up in jail. The penalties for getting behind on child support payments are especially severe. Such debts will remain on your credit report for up to seven years. In most states, you will also be denied an original or renewed driver's license or professional license (for doctors, lawyers, contractors, and so forth) or be at risk of having your current driver's license suspended. If you owe more than $2,500, you may be denied a U.S. passport.

Most important, not keeping up with child support payments could harm your child's well-being by making it difficult for the child's custodial parent to properly provide for him or her. As a parent, you have a responsibility to help care for your child, including financially. "If anyone does not provide for his relatives, and especially for his immediate family, he has denied the faith and is worse than an unbeliever" (1 Timothy 5:8).

If you have tried all of the steps suggested in chapter 3 and still find it impossible to make your alimony or child support payments, try to negotiate with your former spouse for a lower payment. Whether you go to your former spouse first or not, you'll have to work through a court for approval on any changes in the amount you are paying. To succeed, you'll have to demonstrate that your income has decreased substantially and involuntarily (choosing to change to a lower-paid job won't qualify) since the original terms were established or that your expenses have increased, perhaps due to a new child or medical condition.

Changes to the amount you have to pay in alimony or child support cannot be retroactive. Any missed payments must be made up with interest, although the court may approve a payment plan that will bring your payments up to date.

If negotiations fail or the court denies your request, you may be forced into bankruptcy. Bankruptcy won't erase your past, current, or future support obligations, but by canceling other debts, it may free up money to make your support payments.

Free Financial Counseling Advisable

The difficulties discussed in this chapter involve more than financial decisions. The prospect of losing your home, for example, can be a very emotional issue. Mixing a complex financial decision with strong emotions can lead to bad decisions. If you are facing any of these types of decisions, I recommend that you make use of the free financial-counseling services we discussed. A trained credit or housing counselor can provide much needed objective, informed guidance.

WRITE IT ON YOUR HEART

Be joyful in hope, patient in affliction, faithful in prayer. (Romans 12:12)

Chapter 6

When Your Financial Engine Stops Running

The hardest work in the world is being out of work.

— WHITNEY YOUNG, JR.

Losing your job can be a devastating financial experience. It's well and good to talk about building savings and accelerating debt repayment, but if you don't have income, none of that is possible. The emotional devastation this causes only intensifies the difficulty.

When Sam lost his job as one of the pastors at a large church, he was angry. He recalls, "I remember one time when I was running and I had no energy. I couldn't run anymore because I was ticked off at God. I wanted to wrap my hands around his neck and strangle him."

Sam's wife, Susan, acknowledges feeling some anger over the situation as well. "It was a wrestling process. I'd go from being discouraged to being amazed at God's provision." While Sam was out of work, a water pipe in their home broke, flooding their basement. It seemed like trial upon trial. Then the insurance settlement ended up covering not just the basement repairs but a tax bill as well. Susan says, "I remember thinking, 'Doesn't God have a wonderful sense of humor?' You can be so angry at God and yet so awed that he would do something like that. Also, during that season, someone sent us a grocery gift card for a hundred dollars. We said, 'Wow, God, that was amazing.'"

Sam and Susan were better prepared for a financial emergency than many people. She worked, they had some money in reserve, and they didn't have any credit card or vehicle debt. Still, they had one child in college and another finishing high school, so Sam's unemployment compensation didn't stretch nearly far enough. In fact, it hardly covered their newly inflated health insurance premiums of $1,800 per month (more on that coming up). So although Sam would have preferred another pastor's position, he humbled himself and took three part-time jobs: one at a call center, one at a grocery store, and another as a ski instructor. He says, "I went from working for a megachurch to making ten to twelve bucks an hour working alongside teenagers. In part, it was out of financial necessity, but it was also about sanity. I needed to get out of the house and do something."

Sam and Susan also got rigorous about managing expenses, buying only what was necessary. At one point, they thought about selling their home. "We said, 'This is just a house,'" Susan explained. "It's that whole humbling thing. Both Sam and I realized that none of these things—the house we live in, the car we drive—is what makes us who we are. Those things don't hold the value for us that they did twenty years ago."

Today Sam is pastor of another church, and he finds his experience with unemployment comes in handy when counseling others. "I tell them to feel what they're feeling. Sometimes, as Christians, we think we're not supposed to get mad. But you have to be honest. Then you can start putting together a plan for getting back on your feet."

As Sam and Susan's story shows, you can survive a job loss.

A Job-Loss Survival Plan

Let's take a look at what to address if you lose your job.

Unemployment Benefits
Apply for unemployment benefits right away. Most states have a waiting period of up to three weeks before you'll receive your first check, and the

clock starts ticking when you apply, not the day you lose your job.

Regulations vary by state, but generally you will qualify for benefits if you were laid off or otherwise lost your job through no fault of your own. You probably won't qualify if you quit or were fired for willful misconduct, although you may qualify if you were fired for poor performance. Some states provide unemployment benefits for part-time workers who lose their jobs; others do not. Check with your state's unemployment office. The amount of money you have earned and your time on the job also impact whether you qualify and how much assistance you may receive. Last, you must be physically able and available to work and actively seeking employment.

Don't count on unemployment compensation to replace your former income. The national average for unemployment compensation is about three hundred dollars per week, which is taxable income. Benefits typically last up to twenty-six weeks, although the duration is sometimes extended during times of high unemployment.

To find out where to apply, go to www.servicelocator.org/OWSLinks.asp. In some states, you can apply for benefits over the phone or online. Once you start receiving benefits, you'll need to contact the office once a week with an update on your status in order to keep receiving benefits. While you're on your state's unemployment office website, look around. Many offer additional services, including help with résumé writing and tips on interviewing skills.

If you receive a severance package in which your former employer continues paying you on a regular schedule, you may have to wait until that compensation runs out before qualifying for unemployment, but go ahead and apply for benefits. Your state's unemployment office will make the decision. Working part-time while receiving benefits will likely reduce or even eliminate your unemployment compensation.

Some people are hesitant to sign up for unemployment benefits because they think of it as welfare or they're concerned about its impact on their credit score. Unemployment compensation is not welfare. The government doesn't pick up the cost; employers do. No need to worry about your credit score. Drawing unemployment compensation will not have any impact.

Keep in mind that it may make more sense for you to take a temporary part-time job than to draw unemployment compensation. A number of companies even provide health insurance for their part-time workers, including Barnes & Noble, Cost Plus World Market, IKEA, Lands' End, Lowe's, Nike, Nordstrom, REI, Starbucks, Target, Trader Joe's, UPS, Wegmans, and Whole Foods Market. Banks, universities, and hospitals are also good bets when looking for a part-time job with benefits.[1]

Health Insurance

If you had health insurance and worked for a company employing at least twenty people, you should be able to sign up for what's commonly known as COBRA. The name comes from the Consolidated Omnibus Budget Reconciliation Act, legislation designed to prevent employees who are between jobs from losing their group health insurance. You'll usually have sixty days to sign up, and the coverage is retroactive, so you don't have to sign up right away. If you are eligible, the coverage is available for up to eighteen months and can be extended if you become disabled during the first sixty days of coverage.

Health insurance under COBRA is more expensive than when you were an employee — often *much* more expensive — because your former employer is no longer picking up part of the cost. If you have medical conditions that may make it difficult to obtain coverage on your own, you'll probably need to go with the COBRA coverage. However, if you do not have any preexisting conditions, you may be able to do better with an individual policy. Check prices at www.ehealthinsurance.com or find a local health insurance agent through the National Association of Health Underwriters (www.nahu.org).

Be sure to understand policy provisions. When I stepped down from my marketplace job to write and speak full-time, we opted for COBRA *and* paid for another policy through Blue Cross/Blue Shield. We hoped to have another baby and Blue Cross/Blue Shield had a one-year waiting period before maternity coverage kicked in. It was a very expensive year.

You'll qualify for COBRA whether you leave the company by your choice or your employer's choice, unless you're fired for gross misconduct.

One other note about COBRA: A covered employee's spouse may elect COBRA coverage in the event of a divorce that would otherwise cause the spouse to lose health insurance coverage.

Retirement Savings

If you have money in an employer-sponsored retirement plan, roll the money over into a traditional individual retirement account (IRA) at a brokerage house, such as Vanguard (www.vanguard.com) or Fidelity (www.fidelity.com). Most of the big brokerage houses make it easy for you to do this. You'll find information on their websites.

If you get another job quickly, you can roll the money into your new employer's plan. However, you'll have more investment options if you roll the money into a brokerage house IRA. Technically, you could also take a lump-sum distribution from your plan, but that's generally the worst option. Unless you put the money into an IRA or a new employer's retirement plan within sixty days, you'll end up owing taxes on the money and, if you are under age fifty nine and a half, a 10 percent early-distribution penalty.

One final option is that you may be able to leave the money right where it is, in your former employer's retirement plan, as long as you meet your employer's minimum-balance requirement. However, the greater variety of investment options you'll have by rolling the money into a brokerage house IRA makes a rollover the better option.

If you roll the money into a traditional IRA you won't have to pay taxes on it. You can't roll the money directly into a Roth IRA. In order to get the money into a Roth IRA, you will have to first roll it into a traditional IRA and then convert it into a Roth IRA. However, you will owe income taxes.

Expenses

You'll want to be as rigorous as possible in controlling expenses, so review your *Monthly Cash Flow Plan* and eliminate all unnecessary expenses.

If you don't have sufficient emergency-fund savings, your mortgage or rent payment may quickly become a stress point. If you own your own home and anticipate having trouble making the mortgage payment, let your lender know. Ideally, you may qualify for a forbearance, which, as we discussed in the last chapter, is a temporary period in which you can stop making payments or pay only the interest charges. Once you're working again, you'll need to add the missed payments to future payments.

If you have other debts that you may not be able to pay, get in touch with your creditors. If you have student loans, you may be eligible for a deferment or forbearance. If you have a vehicle loan, you may be able to skip a payment that you'll make up later. If you have credit card debts, call your credit card companies and ask about the options that might be available to you under their hardship programs.

A Word to the Employed

If you have a job, there is no guarantee of future employment, but there's a lot you can do to shore up future employability. Most large employers offer some type of educational assistance, yet fewer than 10 percent of eligible employees take advantage of such programs.[2] Does your employer offer tuition reimbursement or training opportunities? If so, take part. Staying up to date with the latest thinking in your field is one of the most productive steps you can take toward securing your future employment. Even checking out and reading the latest books about your field from the library will help you stay current.

Networking helps as well. It's much better to have a network to turn to if you lose your job than to have to build one from scratch. The website www.linkedin.com is a good online career networking tool.

Local meetings of your alumni association or trade associations related to your field are also good places to build a professional network.

WRITE IT ON YOUR HEART

Do not be anxious about anything, but in everything, by prayer and petition, with thanksgiving, present your requests to God. (Philippians 4:6)

Chapter 7

Tapping Your Reserves

In the house of the wise are stores of choice food and oil,
but a foolish man devours all he has.

— PROVERBS 21:20

In tough financial times it can be tempting to tap into the equity in your home, the money in a retirement account, or a life insurance policy. And it's relatively easy to access that money. But should you? Maybe, but probably not.

Before you dip into such funds, take a hard look at whether doing so may amount to throwing good money after bad. Will it help you through a short-term problem, giving you the breathing room you need to get to a better place? Or could it just prolong your difficulties? Even worse, could it get you into even more trouble?

One study found that two-thirds of borrowers who took out a home equity loan to pay off credit card debt racked up more credit card debt within two years.[1] So before considering the options in this chapter, make sure you've addressed the root causes of your financial problems. For instance:

- Have you assessed what led to your difficulties?
- Do you have a couple of accountability partners who are walking with you through the process of resolving those problems?
- Are you using the *Monthly Cash Flow Plan* to guide your day-to-day spending?

If you are having a tough time paying your bills, I recommend that you get rigorous about managing expenses, increasing income, and exploring the other options discussed in the preceding chapters before depleting the equity in any assets you own.

If you really can't afford your home, using money earmarked for your later years in order to prevent foreclosure may lead you to lose your home *and* jeopardize your retirement. If you are tempted to trade high-interest credit card debts for a home equity loan, you may only make your situation worse by putting your home at risk.

In 2007, American homeowners' percentage of equity in their homes fell below 50 percent for the first time since 1945, when the Federal Reserve began tracking home equity. The drop in equity, which has left more people than ever entering retirement still saddled with mortgage debt, was due in no small part to people tapping the equity in their homes through the methods we are about to discuss.

So be forewarned: I'm not a fan of treating your home like a piggy bank. But let's look at some of the options, nonetheless.

Four Ways to Borrow Against Your Home Equity

There are four ways to borrow against the equity in your home: a home equity loan (HEL), a home equity line of credit (HELOC), cash-out refinancing, and a reverse mortgage.

Home Equity Loans

These are closed-end loans, meaning you agree to pay back the borrowed money in equal monthly payments within a set period of time. They are generally fixed-rate loans with terms ranging from five to fifteen years. You borrow the money all at once and start repaying right away. Closing costs typically range from three hundred to five hundred dollars.

The Dangers of Trading Unsecured Debt for Secured Debt

While writing this book, I received a direct-mail pitch from our mortgage lender, stating, "Money can't buy happiness. But our home equity line of credit can help!" The brochure went on to extol the virtues of paying off high-interest debt and lowering monthly payments.

At first glance, it may sound wise to consolidate the debts you're carrying on one or more high-interest credit cards for lower-cost home equity debt, especially because the interest on home equity loans is often tax deductible. But what the marketing pitches don't point out is that you would be trading unsecured debt for secured debt. Bankruptcy is a last resort for dealing with financial problems. However, if you had to go that route, your unsecured debt, such as credit card and medical debt, could be excused. But if you turn such debts into mortgage debt, you'll lose that option. You'll also be putting your home at risk, as the only way to get out of mortgage debt when filing for bankruptcy is to give back your house.

Nor is it a good idea to pay off student loan debt with a home equity loan, for the same reasons. If you have difficulties making your student loan payments, consider the remedies discussed in chapter 4. If you transfer your student loan debt to a home equity loan, you will lose access to those remedies.

One other common use of home equity loans is for the purchase of vehicles. This is a bad idea. In fact, I am not in favor of financing vehicles through any means. Buying vehicles with cash is the way to go if you want to live with financial margin.

Home Equity Line of Credit

This is open-ended; you tap your home equity via special checks or a credit card when you need the money, drawing against the amount granted when you opened the account. These are typically variable rate loans and usually have terms of ten years. Some require payments that are insufficient to repay the principal by the end of the term, leaving you with a balance due. HELOCs often come with fees for a home appraisal, application, points, and closing costs. Plus, even if you don't tap the credit, you'll usually pay a small annual fee for the privilege of having access to the money.

Cash-Out Refinancing

With cash-out refinancing, you draw out equity that you've paid into the home or that has come about through appreciation. This is not a second mortgage—it's a new mortgage. You'll have to foot the bill for a new appraisal and closing costs. If you're considering this option, watch out that you don't trigger the need for private mortgage insurance, which could happen if you end up with less than 20 percent equity in your home. Also, I'd advise against cash-out refinancing that extends the term of your loan beyond your planned retirement age.

Reverse Mortgage

Also known as a Home Equity Conversion Mortgage, or HECM, a reverse mortgage is another way to borrow against the equity in your home. To qualify for most reverse mortgages, you must be sixty-two or older and own your own home outright or have just a small mortgage balance remaining. Reverse mortgages may be structured a number of ways. You can receive a lump-sum payment, money as needed (similar to a home equity line of credit), monthly payments for a fixed period or as long as you live in your home, or some combination of those options. After you move out or die, the loan is repaid with money from the sale of your house. If the proceeds are insufficient to pay off the loan, the lender absorbs the loss.

Some issues to be aware of regarding reverse mortgages include:

- They typically come with high fees.
- You must keep current on taxes, insurance, and maintenance.
- Such a loan may disqualify you from government benefits, such as Medicaid.
- Potential borrowers are required to go through third-party financial counseling with a counselor approved by the U.S. Department of Housing and Urban Development (HUD). You can find a HECM counselor through the HUD website at www.hud.gov.

You will find additional information about reverse mortgages on HUD's website by searching for "HECM." AARP also has helpful information on the topic at www.aarp.org/money/revmort.

Retirement Savings

Money you've been diligently saving for your later years is surprisingly easy to tap well before retirement. Some employers see this easy access as an incentive to get employees to contribute to their retirement plan. However, just as I don't like the idea of treating your home as an ATM, I'm not in favor of robbing your future to pay for your present. Still, let's look at the options.

Employer Retirement Plans

Many participants in 401(k), 403(b), and 457(b) retirement plans are eligible to take loans against their account balance. At some companies, loan availability may be based on your intended use of the money. Your human resources department or plan administrator will know all the rules and regulations unique to your plan. If a loan is available to you, IRS regulations allow you to borrow up to 50 percent of your vested balance, up to a maximum of fifty thousand dollars.[2] Most loans are for five-year terms, although a loan used to purchase a primary residence may be paid back over a longer period. The interest rate charged is typically relatively low, usually one or two points above the prime rate.

A loan against your retirement plan needs to be repaid, and this introduces the first caution about taking such loans. If you leave your job, by choice or otherwise, the loan will become due, often within thirty to ninety days. If you don't repay the money, the balance is taxed and penalized as an early distribution.

Hardship withdrawals are also available from many workplace retirement plans. If your employer allows for such withdrawals, you typically will be allowed to withdraw up to the amount you have contributed to the plan and possibly any amounts your employer has contributed, but not earnings. Here's the kicker. You will need to pay taxes on the money, and if you are under fifty-nine and a half, you will also owe a 10 percent penalty. In addition, you may not be allowed to contribute to your 401(k) for the next six months.

According to the IRS, a hardship withdrawal is allowed if there is an "immediate and heavy financial need" of the employee, the employee's spouse, or a dependent. Such needs include paying for medical expenses not covered by insurance, preventing foreclosure or eviction from your home, covering funeral expenses, and repairing a primary residence. Oddly, the rules also deem the following to be hardships: The need for money to buy a primary residence or to pay for higher education costs for you, your spouse, your dependents, or children who are not dependents. Those hardly seem like hardships. In fact, the price you'll pay for this money in the form of taxes and penalties will be a greater hardship. If you are thinking of tapping retirement funds to pay for education, whether through a retirement plan loan or hardship withdrawal, explore getting a student loan first. If you need a hardship withdrawal to buy a home, you can't really afford that home.

You can make a hardship withdrawal without financial penalties if:

- You become totally disabled.
- You are in debt for medical expenses that exceed 7.5 percent of your adjusted gross income.
- You are required by court order to give the money to your divorced spouse, a child, or a dependent.
- You leave your employer in the year you turn fifty-five or later because of a permanent layoff, termination, quitting, or taking early retirement.

If you have to choose between a loan and a hardship withdrawal before age fifty-nine and a half, go with the loan. In most cases, a hardship withdrawal will cost you more. A loan, assuming it is paid back according to your retirement plan's guidelines, will not be taxed or penalized.

But I'd be hesitant about tapping retirement account money either way. Even though the money is easy to access (there's no credit check required) and the interest rate is usually relatively low, taking money from your retirement plan will cause you to lose out on the tax-deferred [or tax-free in the case of a Roth 401(k)] earnings your money could generate. Take the example of a person who, beginning at age thirty, contributes $5,000 a year to her 401(k) plan. At age forty, she buys a house and takes a $10,000 hardship withdrawal for the down payment. Let's assume her portfolio generates an average annual return of 8 percent. By the time she's sixty-five, she will have $793,094. Had she not taken the hardship withdrawal, she would have had $861,584, which is $68,490 more. Plus, the loan payments she now has to make may lead her to reduce her monthly plan contributions, only worsening her retirement preparedness.

Traditional IRAs

With a traditional IRA, your money goes in pretax and grows on a tax-deferred basis. You may access the money without penalty beginning at age fifty-nine and a half. However, because the money went in pretax, you have to pay income taxes on the money when you take it out.

If you take money out of a traditional IRA before age fifty-nine and a half, you will typically owe taxes *and* a 10 percent penalty because it will be considered a premature distribution. However, according to IRS regulations, the following hardships qualify for penalty-free (but not tax-free) early distributions:

- Excessive unreimbursed medical expenses
- Payment of medical insurance premiums while unemployed
- Total and permanent disability

IRS rules also allow for penalty-free early distributions for the purchase of a home or to pay qualified education expenses. Up to $10,000 of traditional IRA funds may be used to buy a home, if it's the first home you've ever purchased or you haven't owned a home for the past two years.

As for qualified educational expenses, you, your spouse, your children, or your grandchildren can use traditional IRA money to help cover the costs of attending any accredited college, university, vocational school, or other post-secondary facility that meets federal student aid program requirements. The money can be used to cover the cost of tuition, fees, and supplies. If the student is enrolled at least part-time, the money can also be used for room and board.

There is one other way to tap traditional IRA money before age fifty-nine and a half without penalty. If you meet certain requirements, IRS rules allow you to take a series of "substantially equal periodic payments" for at least five years or until you reach age fifty-nine and a half, whichever comes later. This is known as a 72(t) distribution. You'll find more information on the IRS website at www.irs.gov.

Roth IRAs

With a Roth IRA, your money goes in after-tax and grows on a tax-free basis. When you withdraw the money after age fifty-nine and a half, there are no taxes due.

You may access the money you contributed to a Roth IRA (but not the earnings) without taxes or penalty at any time. If you've had your Roth for at least five years, you can withdraw $10,000 worth of contributions *and* earnings without tax or penalty for a first-time home purchase.

Cash-Value Life Insurance

If you have a cash-value life insurance policy (as opposed to term insurance), a policy that provides a death benefit while also building savings, and no one would need the full death benefit in the event of your death, this may be a source of money you could use to pay off debt or pay bills while unemployed.

There are three ways to access the cash value of your policy: through a loan, by surrendering the policy, or with a life settlement.

A Loan

You may take out a loan that allows you to borrow up to the full cash value of your policy, and you are not even required to pay it back, but you will need to pay interest on the loan. Check with your agent to see if the dividends generated by your policy are enough to cover the interest. Just make sure the loan balance never exceeds the cash value, something that could happen if the dividends are not sufficient to cover the interest on the loan or if you are not making interest payments. If this were to occur, you may risk termination of the policy. When you borrow against the cash value of your policy, your death benefit will be reduced by the amount of the loan. So again, make sure that the reduced death benefit would be sufficient to cover the needs that prompted you to buy life insurance in the first place.

Surrendering the Policy

You could also surrender, or cash out, your policy in order to take the cash value. That way you won't have to worry about making interest payments on a loan. If you cash out your policy, you'll owe income taxes on the amount you receive minus what you paid in premiums and any dividends you received. And, of course, the policy will be canceled.

A Life Settlement

A relatively new option is to sell your policy in what's known as a life settlement. By doing so, you could get more (sometimes far more) than the cash value. This may be an option for you, even if you hold a term life insurance policy, as long as the policy is convertible to a cash-value policy. In that case, you may be able to sell it for more than what the cash value would be upon conversion.

Here's how life settlements work. A buyer purchases the policy from you, continues paying the premiums while you are alive, and then collects the death benefit when you die. They purchase the policy from you for less than the policy's death benefit but more than the cash value. Buyers usually prefer policies with a death benefit of $250,000 or more, held by people who are sixty-five or older. The size of the settlement, which is the amount you sell the policy for, varies. It depends on your age, health, and life expectancy. Typically, policies go for 20 to 30 percent of the death benefit, which is often two and a half times the amount you would get by surrendering your policy for cash.[3]

Of course, Uncle Sam will want his cut. Check with your tax advisor if you're considering this route, as the rules are still being worked out, but here is generally how the taxes would work: You will probably owe ordinary income taxes on the amount of cash value that exceeds how much you have paid in premiums; then you will likely owe capital gains taxes on the amount you receive in excess of the cash value.

Let's say you have a policy with a cash value of $50,000. You've paid $20,000 in premiums and you receive $70,000 in cash for your policy. You'll probably owe income tax on the difference between the $20,000 you've paid in premiums and the cash value, or $30,000. Then you will likely owe capital gains tax on the $20,000 you received above the cash value.

As with taking a loan or cashing out a life insurance policy, don't look at this option if someone in your family might need the money upon your death. But if you have other savings that a surviving spouse could live on and your children are on their own, this option may be worth exploring. To find out more about a life settlement, look for a life settlement broker, which you may be able to find through a financial advisor.

Explore Other Alternatives First

As you can tell, I view the options we've just discussed — especially tapping your home equity or your retirement savings — as options of last resort. If you're in financial pain, they can look like easy solutions.

But if you are to get through the tough times *and* set yourself up for long-term success, you will be better served by exploring all other alternatives first. That means using a *Monthly Cash Flow Plan* to look for ways to be more effective in all expense categories, considering a second job for a season, and talking with your creditors to learn about other repayment options. If you have equity in your home or money saved for your retirement, chances are you've worked hard to build those assets. Don't be quick to throw away all that hard work.

WRITE IT ON YOUR HEART

God is our refuge and strength, an ever-present help in trouble. (Psalm 46:1)

Chapter 8

When All Else Fails

When life knocks you down, try to land on your back.
Because if you can look up, you can get up.

— LES BROWN

*B*ankruptcy is a scary word. It can be even scarier within Christian circles. What about the biblical admonition that "the wicked borrow and do not repay, but the righteous give generously" (Psalm 37:21)? Does that make a person who has filed for bankruptcy, or who is considering filing, a "wicked" person? No. Although bankruptcy should be a last resort (that's why the topic is so far back in this book!), it *is* a viable option, even for a follower of Christ. In fact, you may have no other choice.

Three Important Questions

Consider the following questions to help determine whether bankruptcy is the appropriate next step for you.

Is There No Other Choice?

If you have implemented ideas from chapter 3 and negotiated with your creditors in good faith, only to have them play hardball by garnishing your wages or suing you, making it impossible for you to take care of your family's needs, then bankruptcy may be right for you.

Have You Taken Responsibility for Your Debts?

The one traffic accident I've been in was clearly not my fault. A car coming from the other direction, whose driver didn't have a good view of traffic moving my direction, took a chance and turned right in front of me. I hardly even had time to touch the brake pedal. When the police arrived, they didn't hesitate in issuing the other driver a ticket. But as I worked through the insurance claim in the days ahead, I found out that Illinois law states that unless your vehicle is at a complete standstill when it is in an accident, you have to take some responsibility. The reasoning is that if you were moving, there must have been something you could have done to prevent the accident or at least lessen its severity. I had to accept 15 percent of the responsibility.

The same principle applies here. As we discussed in chapter 2, you may have gone through some difficult circumstances that led to your debts: a divorce, the death of a spouse, medical problems, an extended time of unemployment. Still, chances are you can identify something you could have done to avoid the problems you now face or at least to make them less severe. This isn't about adding insult to injury; it's about owning up to your part in your situation, however small. What could you have done differently?

Have You Taken Steps to Avoid Debt Problems in the Future?

Now that you've identified some aspect of your situation that you can own, what are you doing about it? If you weren't using a budget to manage your spending prior to getting into debt, are you now using one? If any of your debts are credit card debts, have you committed to not using your credit cards, at least for the foreseeable future? Do you have an accountability partner you are willing to meet with on a monthly basis to review your finances?

Before filing for bankruptcy, you should be able to say yes to all three of these questions. The first question is about qualifying for bankruptcy based on your financial circumstances; the second and third questions are about making sure bankruptcy will be more than a short-term solution. An alarming number of people who file for bankruptcy find that even exercising this option of last resort does not turn out to be the solution they were hoping for.

According to the Consumer Bankruptcy Project, a Harvard University–based research group that has studied bankruptcy for twenty years, only half of all bankruptcy filers said their financial situation had improved a year after filing. For 35 percent, their financial situation remained the same, and 15 percent said their situation had actually gotten worse.[1]

Accepting God's Forgiveness

Okay, so now you've decided that bankruptcy makes sense. However, you may still feel hesitant. Perhaps you feel embarrassed or guilty. If so, may I remind you that Scripture contains numerous examples of God forgiving people of all sorts of bad behavior. For instance, Jesus forgave prostitutes (see Luke 7:36-50), extortionists (see Matthew 9:9-13), thieves (see Luke 23:26-43), adulterers (see John 8:1-11), and murderers (see Acts 9).

Some biblical money-management teachers say that Christians who file for bankruptcy should still pay back what is owed, even if it takes the rest of their lives. But Jesus didn't say to those he forgave, "Go now, leave your life of sin, *and* show up every Saturday to clean the floors of the temple for the next twenty years." He gave them a fresh start. Likewise, bankruptcy offers a fresh start for those who have gotten themselves into more financial trouble than they can handle, have done all that they can to pay back their debts, and have taken steps to avoid such trouble in the future.

A Bankruptcy Short Course

The most common types of bankruptcy for individuals are Chapter 7 and Chapter 13, named for sections of the bankruptcy code. Let's start by looking at what's true for both types of bankruptcy and then focus on the unique aspects of each type.

Not All Debts Are Wiped Out

Certain debts and ongoing obligations cannot be wiped out through bankruptcy. For example, you'll need to keep making child support and alimony payments. If you are past due with such support, you'll need to catch up; such debts are never dischargeable. Student loans are forgiven only in rare situations, such as when your financial problems make it impossible to maintain a minimal living standard and your difficulties are likely to continue. Many tax debts are not dischargeable. As for homes and vehicles you want to keep, often you will need to continue making payments according to the terms of your contracts.

Credit Counseling Required

Within the six-month period prior to your filing for bankruptcy, you must complete credit counseling in order to determine whether you really need to go through bankruptcy. If you end up filing, you will also have to take part in a personal-money-management course. To find an approved counseling agency or money-management-course provider, go to the U.S. Department of Justice website (www.usdoj .gov/ust) and click on "Credit Counseling & Debtor Education." Many credit-counseling offices affiliated with the National Foundation for Credit Counseling are also approved for such counseling and courses.

Collection Activities Cease

Filing for bankruptcy stops most debt collectors from contacting you. It also means that your creditors may not sue you or move ahead with a pending lawsuit, record liens against your property, seize your property, or garnish your wages to pay your debts. Foreclosure proceedings are also stopped, at least initially. However, in many cases, such proceedings eventually will be allowed to continue unless you file for a chapter 13 bankruptcy.

If you are renting and haven't been paying your rent, many bankruptcy judges will usually allow the landlord to continue with eviction proceedings.

Utility companies can't shut off your service because you filed for bankruptcy. However, if you don't give them a deposit or other means to assure future payment, they can shut off your service soon after you file.

Now let's look at the unique features of the two main types of personal bankruptcy.

Chapter 7

Chapter 7 is known as liquidation bankruptcy. You give up certain assets, which are sold in order to pay as much of your unsecured debt (credit card debt, medical debt, and so on) as possible. Ninety-five percent of Chapter 7 filers don't wind up having to give up any property. They either don't own much, or what they do have is protected—or exempt—under bankruptcy law.[2]

Exemptions vary by state. In some states, only a small amount of home equity is exempt from creditors. If you live in one of those states and are among the few filers who have a lot of equity in your home, the bankruptcy trustee may take possession of the home, sell it, and use the nonexempt portion of the equity to pay your creditors. In other states, such as Florida and Texas, the amount of equity that a person going through bankruptcy can keep is much higher. However, even in those two states, relatively new federal exemption rules put caps on the amount of home equity that can be kept if you purchased your home within forty months of your bankruptcy filing. If your home equity is exempt and you want to keep your home, you'll have to keep making mortgage payments. If you've fallen behind on your payments, it's up to your mortgage company to decide if it is willing to work with you in coming up with a repayment plan.

Retirement accounts—such as a 401(k) or an IRA as well as Social

Security, unemployment, and disability income—are federally exempt in bankruptcy. You'll find more exemption information at www.bank ruptcyaction.com (click on "Bankruptcy Exemptions").

Whatever unsecured debts remain will be forgiven, except for the debts mentioned earlier in this chapter, such as delinquent alimony and child support, student loan debt, and many tax debts.

To determine whether you qualify to file under Chapter 7, see how your average monthly income from the last six months compares with the median for your household size in your state. You can find median income tables by state and family size at the website of the United States Trustee, www.usdoj.gov/ust (click on "Means Testing Information"). If your income is below the median, you can file for Chapter 7; if not, you must take a means test.

The means test figures out whether you have enough disposable income to repay at least a portion of your unsecured debts over a five-year repayment period. It looks at your income and then subtracts IRS-determined amounts for living expenses (food, clothing, transportation, and so on), priority debts (child support, alimony, taxes, and wages owed to employees), and debt payments on secured debts (cars, homes). If what's left over is less than a hundred dollars, you will be allowed to file for Chapter 7; if not, you may have to file under Chapter 13. You can use an online calculator (www.legalconsumer.com) to see how you fare with the means test.

Disabled veterans whose debts were incurred during active duty, even if their income would otherwise force them to file under Chapter 13, are allowed to file under Chapter 7.

If you would like to keep some nonexempt property that you would otherwise have to surrender, you may be able to do so by redeeming the item. That means buying it from the lien holder for its retail value, as long as the lien holder agrees. The retail value for a car, for example, will be listed in the Kelley Blue Book.

You also may be able to keep certain assets by signing a reaffirmation agreement with your creditor. By doing so, you're stating that you'll continue to make payments on the debt even after all your other debts are written off.

It usually takes three to six months to complete a Chapter 7 bankruptcy.

Chapter 13

Chapter 13 is known as reorganization bankruptcy. It is also known as wage-earner bankruptcy because you need to have a regular income in order to qualify. With this type of bankruptcy, you set up a court-approved plan to repay some or all of your debts over three to five years. By law, your payments to creditors under Chapter 13 may not be less than what they would have been under Chapter 7. You usually will not have to give up any property.

With Chapter 13, you make monthly payments to the bankruptcy court, which then divvies up your payment to your creditors. You must devote all of your disposable income (defined as your average monthly income from the past six months, minus monthly expense amounts as allowed by the bankruptcy code) to the plan. Some creditors, such as a former spouse to whom you owe alimony or child support, are entitled to receive all of what you owe; others may end up receiving less than what you owe.

Chapter 13 can be especially helpful to homeowners who have fallen behind on their payments. In fact, Chapter 13 was designed with foreclosure problems in mind. A Chapter 13 filing will stop foreclosure proceedings and can force the lender to accept a plan in which you make up the missed payments through the three-to-five-year bankruptcy repayment plan.

Don't Ruin a Relationship

There is one type of creditor whom you should make every effort to repay: friends and family members who have loaned you money. By law, you are required to list all of your liabilities when you file for bankruptcy, so individual creditors will be included in your formal filing. They may receive at least partial repayment through the formal bankruptcy process. For example, if you file under Chapter 7, they would be among the creditors entitled to a portion of the proceeds generated from the court-ordered liquidation of some of your assets. If you file under Chapter 13, your creditors would be included in your repayment plan. However, in either case, it's unlikely they would end up receiving the full amount you owe. In a Chapter 7 filing, they may end up receiving nothing. Therefore, you should repay whatever portion of the loan they do not recover as part of the bankruptcy process, even if that means paying a small amount each month over a long period of time. Otherwise, your relationship with the person is likely to suffer.

Taking the Next Step

Bankruptcy is a complex procedure involving a mix of federal and state laws. While some people opt for a do-it-yourself bankruptcy, you will probably be better off working with an attorney who specializes in bankruptcy law. A referral from an attorney you know is often the best way to find a good bankruptcy lawyer. If you need more help, the American Board of Certification's website at www.abcworld.org lists attorneys certified as bankruptcy specialists, and the National Association of Consumer Bankruptcy Attorneys' website (www.nacba.org) lists attorneys who specialize in bankruptcy but may not be certified.

The primary downside to working with a bankruptcy lawyer is the cost, an ironic and hard reality for people struggling with their bills. The average attorney's fee for a Chapter 7 bankruptcy case is more than a thousand dollars. For a Chapter 13 case, the average fee is three thousand dollars. In addition, filing fees average about three hundred dollars for each type.[3] In Chapter 13 filings, legal fees can be paid as part of the filer's debt-repayment plan. In Chapter 7 filings, attorneys will sometimes work out payment plans with their clients.

If your income is low, you may qualify for free or low-cost assistance via Legal Service Corporation (LCS), a government-funded program under which free legal services are provided through nine hundred offices around the country. To find an office near you, go to www.lcs .gov and click on "Find Legal Assistance." You might also check with a law school near you to see if pro bono assistance is available.

Two good sites for more information about bankruptcy are the American Bankruptcy Institute website at www.abiworld.org (click on "Consumer Bankruptcy Center) and www.thebankruptcysite.com.

Rebuilding Credit After Bankruptcy

Bankruptcy is by far the most damaging thing you can do to your credit score. Credit bureaus typically report Chapter 7 bankruptcies on your credit report for up to ten years and Chapter 13 bankruptcies for up to seven years.

In order to rebuild your credit score, you'll need to use credit. You will probably be surprised at how soon you start getting credit card offers after completing your bankruptcy. Credit card companies see a lot of upside in that you have filed for bankruptcy. They assume you are likely to carry a balance on your credit cards, and they know that you'll be prohibited from filing for bankruptcy again for another eight years.

If you have difficulty getting a traditional credit card, apply for a secured card in which you deposit a sum of money, which becomes your credit limit. Barry Paperno, Consumer Operations Manager for Fair Isaac Corporation, says the FICO credit scoring formula does not distinguish between secured and unsecured cards. What matters is that you pay your bills on time and don't max out your credit utilization (try to keep charges as low as possible— 10 percent of your available credit or less is best).[4]

You'll probably have to pay an annual fee for a secured card.

Whether you obtain a traditional credit card or a secured card, make a firm commitment to pay your bills on time. That's the most important factor in determining your score. Of course, pay your balance in full as well. Despite many articles to the contrary, you don't need to carry a balance on your cards to improve your credit score; you just need to use the card.

One somewhat controversial option for rebuilding credit is to be added to someone else's card as an authorized user. Even though you would benefit from any positive credit history that person has established, you also have no control over that card. If the person makes a late payment, you'll be penalized. For that reason, I don't recommend becoming an authorized user on someone else's account.

One more step in rebuilding your credit is to review your credit reports from each of the credit bureaus: Experian, TransUnion, and Equifax. You are entitled to one free report per year from each bureau. The only place to go for free reports is www.annualcreditreport.com. Once you have your reports, check for inaccurate information on them, such as accounts that were not included in your bankruptcy filing that are reported as being included or vice versa, and file a dispute to get them corrected. Instructions for filing a dispute will be included with your reports.

For more information about credit scores, check out www.myfico .com.

Avoid "Credit-Repair" Companies

If you're tempted by advertisements promoting credit repair, resist the temptation. The Federal Trade Commission states that it has never seen a legitimate credit-repair company. Such companies claim to be able to erase people's credit score black marks, even if they're valid. That's simply false advertising.[5]

Staying on the Right Track

Of course, smoothing out the financial road ahead involves more than just rehabilitating your credit score; it also involves developing sustainable, productive money-management habits, which is where we will turn our attention next.

WRITE IT ON YOUR HEART

There is surely a future hope for you, and your hope will not be cut off. (Proverbs 23:18)

Chapter 9

A Money Plan for Any Kind of Weather

It will not do to leave a live dragon out of your plans if
you live near one.

—J.R.R. TOLKIEN, *THE HOBBIT*

When Hurricane Ike blew through Texas in the summer of 2008, one of the most stunning photographs of the aftermath showed an entire neighborhood leveled, with the exception of one house. Up and down the street, each house had been flattened, but somehow one house remained standing. It hardly even looked damaged.

When I saw that picture, I thought of the parable of the wise and foolish builders:

Everyone who hears these words of mine and puts them into practice is like a wise man who built his house on the rock. The rain came down, the streams rose, and the winds blew and beat against that house; yet it did not fall, because it had its foundation on the rock. But everyone who hears these words of mine and does not put them into practice is like a foolish man who built his house on sand. The rain came down, the streams rose, and the winds blew and beat against that house, and it fell with a great crash. (Matthew 7:24-27)

As I'm writing these words, there are some fierce economic rains falling, streams rising, and winds blowing. Lots of people's homes are falling, metaphorically and literally, through foreclosure. Even if by the time you read these words the financial storms have calmed down, chances are good they'll return at some point. That's the nature of our economy. It has its ups and downs. But if we build our financial homes on the solid foundation of God's Word, they will stand strong.

Start with the Right Orientation

Once we have some money, we can do only three things with it: spend it, save it, or give it away. That's the order our culture encourages: spend, save, and then give. This approach always seems to come with consumer debt. When spending is your first priority, you never seem to have enough (see Ecclesiastes 5:10), so carrying a balance on your credit cards and financing cars seems normal, unavoidable. But God calls us to the opposite approach: give, save, and then spend. His Word contains strong cautions against the use of debt.

This simple approach—give, save, spend—is rare, yet it's incredibly effective. If you orient your finances this way, being generous with the first portion of all that you receive—saving the next portion and then building your lifestyle on what remains, being sure not to carry a balance on your credit cards or finance cars—you will build a strong financial house equipped to withstand any type of economic weather. Let's look at each element of this approach in more detail.

Make Generosity Your Highest Financial Priority

God doesn't need our money. After all, he made everything, and he still owns everything. Lest we ever forget that, he reminds us: "If I were hungry I would not tell you, for the world is mine, and all that is in it" (Psalm 50:12). How's that for a clearly articulated lack of need? Yet God instructs us to make the financial support of his purposes our highest financial priority: "Honor the LORD with your wealth, with the firstfruits of all your crops" (Proverbs 3:9). Why would God, who doesn't need our money, teach us to send the first portion of all we receive his way? Because he wants our hearts.

When Jesus described the devotion required of anyone who wants to follow him, he cautioned that money would be his chief rival for our hearts (see Matthew 6:24). Giving to God-honoring causes out of the first portion of all we receive is the most tangible financial expression that our highest priority is our relationship with Christ. Those causes include spreading the gospel (see Matthew 28:19-20), the alleviation of suffering among the poor (see Proverbs 19:17, Matthew 25:40), and the support of those who teach God's Word (see Galatians 6:6).

You and I are also on the list of causes God cares about. That becomes clear just by reading past Proverbs 3:9 to Proverbs 3:10, where we discover what will happen after we give to God the first portion of all we receive: "Your barns will be filled to overflowing, and your vats will brim over with new wine." Several other passages of Scripture make this unmistakable promise that we will be rewarded for our generosity:

"Bring the whole tithe into the storehouse, that there may be food in my house. Test me in this," says the LORD Almighty, "and see if I will not throw open the floodgates of heaven and pour out so much blessing that you will not have room enough for it. I will prevent pests from devouring your crops, and the vines in your fields will not cast their fruit," says the LORD Almighty. "Then all the nations will call you blessed, for yours will be a delightful land," says the LORD Almighty. (Malachi 3:10-12)

One man gives freely, yet gains even more; another withholds unduly, but comes to poverty. A generous man will prosper; he who refreshes others will himself be refreshed. (Proverbs 11:24-25)

Give, and it will be given to you. A good measure, pressed down, shaken together and running over, will be poured into your lap. For with the measure you use, it will be measured to you. (Luke 6:38)

Whoever sows sparingly will also reap sparingly, and whoever sows generously will also reap generously. (2 Corinthians 9:6)

These remarkable promises have been twisted into a give-to-get approach to generosity so prevalent it's been branded as its own gospel: the Prosperity Gospel. So although we should be encouraged by these verses, we also need to be careful to understand them. It's tempting to turn them into a spiritual guide to lottery riches, but that is not God's intent. The apostle Paul points out how ridiculous it is to think that we could bribe God with our giving: "Who has ever given to God, that God should repay him?" (Romans 11:35). In other words, God is the giver. He gave us life; he gave us his Son; he gave us all we have.

Giving is a tangible reminder to ourselves that God is our Provider, as King David expressed so well: "Who am I, and who are my people, that we should be able to give as generously as this? Everything comes from you, and we have given you only what comes from your hand" (1 Chronicles 29:14). Giving to get is manipulation; giving out of gratitude is worship. Those I know who give with hearts full of gratitude for how much God has done for them report that they have received something back for their generosity. Some trace material blessings to their giving. Others tell of a closer relationship with Christ, a greater freedom regarding their possessions, and more peace. The most consistent benefit I've witnessed (and experienced) is a heightened sense of joy, which is as Jesus said it would be: "It is more blessed to give than to receive" (Acts 20:35). So the first part of a money plan that will withstand any kind of weather is to be generous.

Base your giving on a percentage of your income (see 1 Corinthians 16:2). If your income decreases, the amount of money you give may decrease, but the percentage will stay the same. By the same token, if your income increases, the amount of money you give will increase while the percentage stays the same.

Aim for giving 10 percent of your income as a starting point because that's the historical biblical starting point (see Genesis 14:20). Then keep increasing the amount. Every example of generosity from the New Testament goes beyond 10 percent (see Mark 12:41-43; Luke 19:1-10).

There are countless needs in the world. As we use what God has entrusted to us to be a blessing to others, we will increasingly understand what Jesus meant when he said it is more blessed to give than to receive.

Savings is the second element in a financial approach that will be able to withstand all kinds of weather.

Make Savings Your Second-Highest Priority

God encourages us to maintain a reserve (see Proverb 21:20). While some may go too far with savings (see Luke 12:16-21), most of us could stand to go a bit further, as Solomon pointed out in what Oprah might call a "smack-down" to someone who was not being wise in their use of money:

> Go to the ant, you sluggard;
>> consider its ways and be wise!
> It has no commander,
>> no overseer or ruler,
> yet it stores its provisions in summer
>> and gathers its food at harvest. (Proverbs 6:6-8)

This principle of storing some provisions dates back thousands of years. In the book of Genesis, for example, we read of Joseph foreseeing seven years of abundance, to be followed by seven years of famine. He encouraged Pharaoh to prepare. And so during the seven years of abundance, a portion of the crops were set aside for the coming lean years (see Genesis 41).

We can't predict when financial famines will come, but we would be wise to assume that they will. Between 1948 and 2001, our economy endured ten recessions, which lasted an average of eleven months a piece and resulted in the loss of billions of dollars.[1] The economy moves in cycles, and so do our households, which can include periods of unemployment or even disability. We need to be prepared for these tough times by setting aside a portion of all we receive.

Here are the types of provisions to gather and maintain.

If Savings

This is your emergency fund. It's what you will live on if your job disappears tomorrow. It's how you'll pay for that medical procedure that's not covered by insurance. I used to believe we should maintain three to six month's worth of living expenses in such an account. Now I believe six month's worth should be the minimum. Less than one in five households has that much money in reserve,[2] which is why economic downturns cause so much financial pain and fear. During the tumultuous economy of the fall of 2008, people with six months' worth of living expenses in an emergency fund were much more likely to report feeling at ease than those with less in savings.[3] Build a reserve of six months' worth of living expenses and you will be unusually well positioned to weather life's ups and downs.

If you don't have an emergency fund, or if your emergency fund totals less than six months' worth of living expenses, make it your highest savings priority to create such a reserve. The only exception is if you have consumer debt (a balance on your credit cards or vehicle loans). In that case, establish an *If* savings account of one month's worth of living expenses, accelerate your debt payments, and then, once you've paid off your consumer debts, build your *If* savings account to six months' worth of living expenses.

Keep this money in a bank (online or traditional) or credit union savings or money market account.

Making Sure Your Money Is Safe

There's nothing like the failure of a bank or other financial institution to drive financial fear. Here's what you need to know about the safety of money saved or invested at various institutions.

Banks. One of the most important indicators that your bank account money is safe is that the Federal Deposit Insurance Corporation (FDIC) insures it. Look for the FDIC symbol on your bank's website. If you can't find it, go to the FDIC's website at www.fdic.gov, click on the "Deposit Insurance" tab, and search for your bank to see if it's protected by the FDIC. You'll also see a calculator that will help you determine how much of the money you have on deposit is protected.

The FDIC used to insure up to $100,000 per depositor per insured bank, which includes the total of money you have in checking, savings, money market accounts, and certificates of deposit. In the case of joint accounts, each co-owner had $100,000 of coverage. Money held in one or more IRAs at a bank was insured for a total of up to $250,000. However, the FDIC insurance limits were temporarily increased at the end of 2008 (until the end of 2009) to $250,000 per depositor per insured bank. In the case of a joint account, the limits for each co-owner were raised to $250,000. IRA insurance limits remain at $250,000. Check the FDIC website to keep up with the latest coverage amounts.

Credit unions. If you have money in a credit union, make sure it is insured by the National Credit Union Share Insurance Fund (NCUSIF) (www.ncua.gov/ShareInsurance) or by American Share Insurance (ASI) (www.americanshare.com).

The NCUSIF covers up to $100,000 held by an individual across checking, savings, or money market accounts or CDs (a two-person joint account is insured at $100,000 per person) or $250,000 in IRAs. ASI covers up to $250,000 for each account held by an ASI-insured credit union member.

Brokerage houses. If you have money at a brokerage house, make sure the Securities Investor Protection Corporation (SIPC) protects it. The SIPC does not protect against investment losses, but it does protect up to $500,000 in brokerage accounts per investor in cases of fraud or the failure of a brokerage house. If you don't see SIPC on your firm's website, search the SIPC's member database at www.sipc.org and click on "Who We Are" and then "Member Database."

Money market mutual funds. Whereas money market accounts are a type of insured savings account offered by banks and credit unions, money market funds are mutual funds, which until the end of 2008 were not insured against investment loss. Historically, money market funds have been extremely safe places to keep savings. However, in September of 2008, for only the second time in history, a money market fund's share price fell below one dollar. There was much concern and many people took money out of money market funds, so the Treasury Department introduced a temporary program that insures investors in such funds against investment losses. Money market funds have to choose to participate in the program, but fairly quickly, all the major fund families joined.

The Federal Reserve's insurance program for money market mutual funds covers only money invested in such funds as of September 19, 2008.

I feel comfortable using money market funds, and do so. However, if the added risk of using a money market fund for your emergency-fund will keep you up at night, put your emergency fund money in a bank or credit union savings account.

When Savings

There are three types of *When* savings:

Near-term *When* **savings.** This type of savings is for items you plan to purchase within the next five years. It also includes bills due less often than monthly, such as a semiannual property tax bill or an annual life insurance bill, and expenses that occur less frequently than monthly, such as home and car maintenance, gifts, and vacations. Identify each such item on your *Monthly Cash Flow Plan*, estimate the annual amount that you spend on each one, divide by twelve, enter that amount in the "Goal" column of your *Monthly Cash Flow Plan*, and each month put the total of each of those amounts into a separate savings account tagged for such items.

In our household, we do this with money allotted for our property taxes, life insurance, homeowners insurance, vehicle insurance, and vacations. Income is deposited into our checking account. Then, once a month, one-twelfth of the annual amount for the total of all of these items is transferred to a separate savings account. When we need that money for one of those bills or to pay for a vacation, we transfer the needed funds to our checking account. For home maintenance, vehicle maintenance, and gifts, we allow money allocated for such items to accumulate in our checking account. We use money for those purposes often enough that it's easiest to allow that money to accumulate in our checking account and use it as needed.

Mid-term *When* **savings.** Money for big-ticket items that will eventually need to be replaced, such as a car or the roof of your home, should be placed in mid-term *When* savings. I recommend that you maintain a separate savings account into which you deposit a lump sum each month earmarked for all such items.

Long-term *When* **savings.** This type of savings holds money for your later years, your kids' college expenses, and possibly a wedding. People get especially concerned about this category of savings during economic downturns. They panic as they see their retirement accounts losing big portions of value.

Here's how to set up your long-term *When* savings to weather such storms:

- *Diversify.* Of course, there was no New York Stock Exchange in Solomon's time, but he may have been the first one to recognize one of the most important principles of wise investing, when he gave the following advice: "Give portions to seven, yes to eight, for you do not know what disaster may come upon the land" (Ecclesiastes 11:2). Modern translation? Spread your money around.

  To be precise, Solomon was talking about generosity, encouraging people to give a portion of what they could to seven or eight people in need. His reasoning was that someday *you* may be the one in need, and the more people you help, the more likely it is that one of those people will be willing and able to help you. The same principle applies to investing. If we put some money in stocks and some in bonds, when the stocks are struggling, the bonds may be able to help us and vice versa.

  So the first step in creating a solid investment portfolio is to diversify your investments. For most people, the best way to do that is to invest in mutual funds, not individual stocks. Mutual funds are inherently diversified, holding hundreds of individual stocks, bonds, and other securities. But there are many types of mutual funds (stock funds, bond funds, international funds, real estate funds, and so on) and numerous companies that sell them. So which ones should you invest in?

Warren Buffet, chairman of Berkshire Hathaway and one of the most successful investors ever, said that index funds are the best way to invest in the stock market for those folks who don't invest as part of their full-time job.[4] An index fund holds a portfolio of securities that closely matches an established index, such as the S&P 500.

- *Allocate.* Even narrowing our choices to index funds still leaves us with a lot of choice, among them *total stock market index funds*, which hold small portions of every publicly traded company in the U.S., and *global index funds*, which include stocks outside the U.S. There are also *bond index funds* and many other types of index funds. Choosing how to diversify with the proper mix of investments—asset allocation—is one of the most important factors in a person's investing success.

In general, with long-term goals, you'll achieve the best return with a higher percentage of your money invested in stock-based index funds. With a short-term goal, you'll need to be more conservative, with a higher percentage of your money invested in bond funds. But many people don't get this allocation right. In one study of 401(k) plan participants, 16 percent of those under age thirty had no holdings in stocks.[5] These investors are being far too conservative. In another study, 27 percent of 401(k) participants age fifty-six to sixty-five had 90 percent of their holdings in stocks.[6] They are being far too aggressive.

The easiest way for you to have and maintain the proper

asset allocation—especially when investing for a long-term goal, such as retirement or your children's college tuition—is to use mutual funds designed with the date of your goal in mind. Most of the big mutual fund companies now offer *target-date mutual funds*. These funds design their asset allocation around the length of time you have to accomplish your goal. If you were twenty years old in the year 2010 and planned to leave the paid workforce at age sixty-five, you would choose a fund with the year 2055 in its name. This fund would likely be mostly invested in stocks, probably a mix of domestic and international stocks. It would be an aggressive allocation based on the fact that you have a long time to work with, so you should be able to ride out the ups and downs of the economy in order to try to achieve a high return on your money. As you get older, the fund will automatically shift its asset allocation to a more conservative mix, since you have less time to ride out the economy's ups and downs. If you were fifty-five years old in the year 2010 and just beginning to invest for your retirement, you would choose a target-date fund that has the year 2020 in its name, which would likely have a lower portion of its investments in the stock market and a higher portion in more conservative securities. However, if you were just starting to invest for your later years at age fifty-five, you would likely be better off planning to wait until age seventy or so before stepping out of the paid workforce. You will likely need more time to save for your retirement. In that case, you would choose a target-date fund with the year 2025 in its name.

You can apply the same principle toward saving for a child's future tuition costs. If you are using a 529 college savings plan (learn more at www.savingforcollege.com), which I recommend. You will be able to choose an age-based plan oriented around the current age of your child. For example, because each of our three children is currently under age six, we have their college savings accounts in funds designed for children in that age group.

• *Invest a little at a time.* There's another principle from the Bible that can guide us toward a wise approach to investing: "He who gathers money little by little makes it grow" (Proverbs 13:11). Modern translation? Invest for long-term goals with dollar-cost averaging. That means putting a percentage of your income into your investment account on a regular interval, such as once a month, preferably automatically. In an ideal world, we'd all make our investments when the market is down and take our money out when the market is up ("buy low, sell high"), but we don't live in an ideal world. No one can predict the market. The best we can do is put a portion of our income into our mutual funds on a regular basis.

• *Stay in the game.* The stock market is the only place I know of that when the product (stocks) goes on sale, very few people are interested in buying. To be sure, it takes discipline and a measure of courage to stay the course when the market is in decline, but it's best to do that. That's because there are an amazingly small number of up days that account for most of the gains. For example, between January 1998 and December 2007, the S&P 500 gained an average of 5.9 percent per year. Although that may not be very impressive, consider this: If you did not have money invested in the market during the decade's ten best trading days, your average return would have been just 1.1 percent. If you had been on the sidelines during the decade's twenty best trading days, your average annual return would have been negative 2.6 percent. Had you missed out on the forty best days, you would have lost more than 8 percent per year.[7] The lesson is that you have to stay invested if you are to take advantage of those days.

When the Game Is Short

What if you are close to retirement age and you haven't saved enough or the market takes a sudden hit, leaving you ill-equipped to retire? Don't despair; there are steps you can take.

1. Delay your retirement. I know, you were probably eager to move on to other things. But if you don't have the funds, continuing to work will be your best option. A study from T. Rowe Price found that staying with your full-time job could boost your investment income by 7 percent or more for each additional year of work. For someone who saves 15 percent of his or her salary, working an additional five years, say from age sixty-two to sixty-seven, could raise annual income from investments by 39 percent.[8] Plus, if you work longer, your employer may continue providing health insurance, prescription drug, and other benefits. Continuing to work is not such a bad thing. In fact, studies show that people who stay engaged in meaningful activities in their later years are happier and healthier.[9]

2. Use your Monthly Cash Flow Plan to free up some additional money to save each month. I have yet to meet anyone who couldn't improve their spending effectiveness. Freeing up small amounts of money in a lot of spending categories can add up to a lot of money.

3. Hold off on taking Social Security benefits as long as you can. By delaying your retirement, you may be able to push back the date when you begin taking Social Security benefits. If you qualify for Social Security income, you are eligible to begin receiving that income at age sixty-two. However, waiting until your "full retirement age" (between sixty-five and sixty-seven, depending on the year you were born) will significantly boost your monthly Social Security income. Waiting until age seventy will boost it even further. You can run your own numbers by going to www.socialsecurity.gov and clicking on "Estimate Your Retirement Benefits."

- *Seek wise counselors.* The Bible teaches, "A wise man will hear and increase in learning, and a man of understanding will acquire wise counsel" (Proverbs 1:5, NASB). If you would like some assistance in planning your investments, check out Kingdom Advisors (www.kingdomadvisors.org), an excellent nationwide network of Christian financial advisors.[10] On its site, you can search for a local advisor who has specialized training in investments and in what the Bible teaches about money. Another organization to consider is Everyday Steward. Whereas some financial advisors work with only high-net-worth clients, Everyday Steward works with people regardless of income or net worth, charging a reasonable hourly rate for a variety of services, such as the development of a financial plan. You can learn more at www.everydaysteward.com.

Why Savings

This money is to help fund any dream God has placed on your heart. Maybe you'd like to start your own business someday or create a foundation. If you have a dream you're working toward, it can be helpful to set aside money in a separate savings account to help accomplish the dream. Use the concept of a *Why* savings account if it fits your situation.

Now let's look at the third essential building block for facilitating a solid financial home: spending effectively.

Spending Effectively

In chapter 3, we discussed some ideas for spending more effectively in each of the main expenses categories, so here I want to emphasize the importance of using a *Monthly Cash Flow Plan*. Just 7 percent of households use a detailed plan with specific monthly spending limits in each expense category.[11] A plan will give you the knowledge you need to make any needed adjustments. It's like having lots of levers you can push or pull to navigate whatever economic weather you face.

If you are in financial trouble because of the overuse of credit cards, put the cards away—at least for the foreseeable future and possibly forever. I'm not saying that no one should ever use a credit card; however, some people would be better off not using them, and that may include you. Be honest with yourself. Will the use of credit cards be a stumbling block for you in the future? That's also where having an accountability partner is so important. By meeting with such a friend and showing him or her your financial statements, you'll have a built-in regulator to help you use cards wisely or decide you're better off not using them at all.

Some people believe that using debit cards is safer than credit cards. In some cases, that is true. Just knowing that the card is linked to your checking account may encourage you to spend less; however, it's still possible to spend more than you have with a debit card. Many banks will allow a purchase to go through even when there isn't enough money in your checking account to cover the purchase. When that happens, you'll get hit with an overdraft fee, which has become a huge source of revenue for banks. Therefore, before using your debit card, make sure you have enough money in your account.

Also, beware that some debit cards do not provide the same fraud protection provided by credit cards. With debit cards, fraud coverage depends on how you use your card. Many debit cards can be used two ways: by entering your personal identification numbers (PIN) or by signing for your purchases. Transactions involving a signature come with the same liability protection offered by credit cards, which ranges from zero liability to fifty dollars. With some debit cards, when making PIN-based transactions the same fifty-dollar-limit applies only if fraudulent use is reported within two days. Any later than that and your liability rises to five hundred dollars or higher. Other debit card issuers offer full liability protection. Check with your debit card issuer to find out how much liability protection you have. You may want to sign for your debit card purchases.

Not Enough

The practical ideas covered in this chapter are some of the essential building blocks for a rock-solid financial house, but if our houses are to stand for the long haul, how-to information alone is not enough. If it were, no one would have any financial problems, for there are countless books, websites, magazines, television shows, and radio programs focused on how to manage money well. Yet even as this how-to information has multiplied, our household savings rate has been decreasing and our indebtedness rate has been growing.

We need something more. We need to cultivate the proper attitudes toward money. In the next chapter, we'll talk about the attitudes of the heart that lead to wise money management.

WRITE IT ON YOUR HEART

The plans of the diligent lead to profit as surely as haste leads to poverty. (Proverbs 21:5)

Chapter 10

HABITS OF THE HEART

People need to be reminded more often than they need
to be instructed.

— SAMUEL JOHNSON

The film *Seabiscuit* is the true story of, as owner Charles Howard put it, a racehorse too small, a jockey too big, a trainer too old, and an owner "too dumb to know the difference."[1] It's a story about identity.

When Seabiscuit was born, his first owner didn't think much of him and used him to train others. In order to give the other horses confidence, the jockey riding Seabiscuit would pull back on the reins near the finish line to let another horse win. Seabiscuit was conditioned to lose.

By the time another trainer, Tom Smith, got his first look at Seabiscuit, the horse had become angry and uncooperative. But Smith saw potential in Seabiscuit and persuaded Howard, his boss, to buy the horse. In one powerful scene, Smith and Howard are watching Seabiscuit resist the commands of his jockey as the horse runs this way and that around a track. Sensing Howard's concern, Smith tells him, 'I just can't help feeling they got him so screwed up running in a circle he's forgotten what he was born to do. He just needs to learn how to be a horse again."[2] So they take him to a meadow and let him run. And run he does, fast and free.

Some of us have been so messed up by the messages of our consumer culture that we've forgotten what we were born to do. We've bought into the lies that we don't have enough, that we are not enough, that we need something more in order to be more. We just need to learn how to be children of God again.

Of course, there's nothing wrong with buying things. Biblical money management is not about asceticism or making do with the least expensive car, clothes, or living room couch, but there's a lot that's wrong with looking to such things for our identity, value, and ultimate happiness. When we do, we settle for life on a treadmill of buying and wanting and buying some more. It goes a long way toward explaining why many of us get into trouble with debt.

Remembering who we are—fully loved children of God—is the first and most essential habit of the heart. It's what enables us to understand the other elements of our God-given identity that are so essential for wise money management: trust, contentment, gratitude, and patience.

Trust

In December 2006, as each week brought news of yet another publisher that had decided to take a pass on a book I had left a well-paying corporate job to write, I found myself discouraged and increasingly worried. Was it a colossal mistake to walk away from a good salary and benefits? Had God really called me to write and teach about biblical money management full-time, or was it simply something I wanted to do? Would I be able to provide for my wife and young children?

At the end of one especially discouraging day, Jude and I were driving to the home of some friends for dinner. I was doing my best to hold it together. Knowing how down I was, she reminded me of the question asked in Matthew 7, "If your children ask for bread, which of you would give them a stone? Or if your children ask for a fish, would you give them a snake? Even though you are bad, you know how to give good gifts to your children. How much more your heavenly Father will give good things to those who ask him" (verses 7:9-11, NCV).

The words felt like such a warm embrace that I could not speak. They were at once so reassuring as well as so humbling. In my worry,

I had doubted God's promise to provide for us. Even worse, I had doubted his love for me.

As we talked that night, we agreed there was no guarantee I would ever find a publisher, but there *was* a guarantee that God would provide for our needs. And he did. Five months later, NavPress offered me a book contract, and a year and a half after that, my book *Money, Purpose, Joy* was released. I remember about that time being in a meeting at the publisher's office in Colorado Springs and finding it difficult to focus on the conversation. I couldn't help thinking back on the journey, and I was overwhelmed by God's goodness.

Whenever we find ourselves worrying about something, that's a good time to stop to pray. God's Word encourages us to do so: "Cast all your anxiety on him because he cares for you" (1 Peter 5:7). Have your financial troubles made you forget how much God loves you? Take a minute to remember that the God of the universe—the Creator of heaven, earth, and sea—considers you his child. He knows your needs and he promises to provide for you.

Contentment

Every day of our lives, we are the unwitting recipients of countless messages designed to foster discontentment. The environments we move through have become so embedded with marketing messages, we hardly even notice them. That's what makes them so effective. If we passed a billboard explicitly stating that a certain brand of clothing will make us popular, we'd immediately identify the lie. But the messages are not that explicit; they're woven tightly into the fabric of our everyday experience, which enables them to shape us in ways we don't recognize. For the most part, they leave us feeling that we need something more, which is what makes the following verses seem so out of synch with our daily lives: "Godliness with contentment is great gain. For we brought nothing into the world, and we can take nothing out of it. But if we have food and clothing, we will be content with that" (1 Timothy 6:6-8).

What? Content with only food and clothing? Why, that's down-right un-American! Or so it seems. But do you know what else it is? It's liberating.

Earlier I mentioned that my wife and I just gave away my car. Until it developed the need for cost-prohibitive repair, the car was running fine, but it sure didn't look good. We used to live in a part of Chicago where we had to park it on the street, and it had been hit several times. The week before we moved from that neighborhood, a tree branch fell on the car, denting the roof. Because the cost of repairs would likely amount to more than what the car was worth, we never bothered to fix any of the dents. When I was working in corporate America, I would drive into the parking lot of my office building and pass lots of new cars. Driving the old Camry gave me frequent opportunities to practice contentment.

What helped me the most was reminding myself that the car gave us the financial freedom to build savings targeted toward being able to leave my corporate job one day to write and speak full-time. The more I dwelled on that benefit, the more thankful I felt for a car that was paid off and that didn't cost much to operate. In the process, I saw that gratitude drives contentment and serves as a powerful antidote to our culture's constant encouragement to want something more.

Gratitude

Writer Fulton Oursler had vivid memories of an old woman named Anna, who raised him as a child. When she sat down to eat she would say, "Much obliged, dear Lord, for my vittles." Oursler wondered why she thanked God, pointing out that she would get the food regardless of whether she gave thanks or not.

"Sure, but it makes everything taste better to be thankful," Anna said. "You know, it's a game an old preacher taught me to play. It's about looking for things to be thankful for. Like one day I was walking to the store to buy a loaf of bread. I look in all the windows. There are so many pretty clothes."

"But, Anna, you can't afford to buy any of them!" he interjected.

"Oh, I know, but I can play dolls with them. I can imagine your mom and sister all dressed up in them and I'm thankful. Much obliged, dear Lord, for playing in an old lady's mind."

Many years later, when Anna was dying, Oursler remembered standing by her bedside. "Her old hands were knotted together in a desperate clutch. Poor old woman," he thought. "What had she to be thankful for now? She opened her eyes and looked at me. 'Much obliged, dear Lord, for such fine friends.'"[3]

Being thankful is not about looking at life through rose-colored glasses or putting on an artificial smile no matter what we're going through. According to the Reverend Dr. John Westerhoff, who tells Anna's story in a booklet called *Grateful and Generous Hearts*, gratitude is about viewing all of life as a gift. "Taking nothing for granted, demanding nothing as her due, [Anna] recognized that we come into this world with nothing, we go out with nothing, and in between we are given all we have."[4]

Right now, gratitude may be the last thing you feel. That's where I was in the early part of 2005. I was grieving and worn out from doing the best I could to help my parents through long illnesses that claimed my mother's life in December of 2003 and my father's in November of 2004. At the time, the worship team at our church frequently sang, "Blessed Be Your Name." For a song that includes the lyrics "You give and take away," its up-tempo rhythm always struck me as wrong. I grew to dislike that song. I could not sing along.

With the passing of time, the pain of my parents' deaths has eased. Gradually, my sense of loss has been replaced by gratitude for having had parents I deeply loved and respected. When the worship team sang that song recently, it wasn't until it was over that I realized I had sung all of the lyrics without hesitation.

In the midst of your financial difficulties, can you praise God for the blessings in your life? Look for little things. If you can develop the habit of expressing thanks on a regular basis in the midst of a season of trial, chances are you will hang on to that habit, and a grateful heart is an immense help in managing money well for the long haul.

Patience

Advancements in technology have stunted our willingness to wait. A microwave dinner that takes two minutes to heat leaves us pacing the kitchen floor. A website that does not open instantly seems slow. But patience, of course, is a fruit of the Spirit, and it is an important key to wise money management. Patience enables us to walk away from a high-pressure salesperson and think about a potential purchase a bit longer. Patience enables us to take a long-term view toward saving and investing. Even more important, when we understand the ulti-mate patience God calls us to live with — the patience for heaven — it changes how we view the things of this world.

Much of the consumer mindset flows from the conclusion that this world is all there is and so this life is our one and only shot at happiness. The apostle Paul was mimicking this mindset when he said, "Let us eat and drink, for tomorrow we die" (1 Corinthians 15:32). More than any other, the mistaken belief that "this is it" is what leaves people wanting and spending and going into debt in a never-ending cycle of trying to satisfy a hunger that just won't go away.

C. S. Lewis got at the heart of that hunger when he wrote, "If I find in myself a desire which no experience in this world can satisfy, the most probable explanation is that I was made for another world."[5] When we realize that our deepest longings will not be satisfied on this side of heaven, it frees us from looking to the things we buy for that which they cannot deliver. It enables us to enjoy them as good gifts from our heavenly Father but not as the source of our identity or ulti-mate happiness.

What if you never got the car you want? What if you never got your dream home? Would that be okay? I'm not saying you won't, and I'm not saying to give up on such goals. I'm just suggesting that we strive toward that which truly does satisfy: fostering close relationships with the people in our lives; using our gifts, talents, and passions to make a difference with our lives; and enjoying a strong, growing relationship with God. Those are the purposes for which we were made, and they will be the sources of our greatest joy.

Be Intentional

These habits of the heart—trust, contentment, gratitude, and patience—will not just happen, nor will the habit of embracing our identity as children of God. They will take some tending, some reminding. A friend of mine once pointed out that we don't need a lot of help learning how to damage our relationships, get out of shape, or get into debt. We drift toward such bad habits, with plenty of encouragement from our culture.

In order to cultivate these habits of the heart, be intentional about spending time with God. Read Matthew 7:9-11 again and again. Be awed, as John was, by the notion that the God of the universe considers you to be his child (see 1 John 3:1). Look and see how he has provided for you. Practice contentment by looking for things to be thankful for, such as being stuck at the end of a long line, which gives you the opportunity to practice patience.

To accept the cultural suggestion that you are a consumer is to settle for far too little. You were made in the image of the God of the universe (see Genesis 1:26-27). You were made for a life of good works prepared in advance for you to do (see Ephesians 2:10). You were made to love God and people well (see Matthew 22:36-40). Allow these truths to permeate your heart, and your use of money will become a powerful, productive, joyful, God-glorifying expression of who you were made to be and what you were made to be about. It is the single most important step you can take toward managing money well for the rest of your life.

WRITE IT ON YOUR HEART

Above all else, guard your heart, for it is the wellspring of life.
(Proverbs 4:23)

Chapter 11

USING YOUR EXPERIENCE TO HELP OTHERS

Don't look out only for your own interests, but take an
interest in others, too.

— PHILIPPIANS 2:4 (NLT)

I started playing golf when I was twelve years old. I remember early in my golfing "career" seeing a poster in a gift shop that read, "The key to life, as in golf, is not staying out of the rough but getting out once we're in." I'm not sure I got the bigger point back then. I thought the poster was just about golf. But I get it now. It doesn't take many years of living before we find ourselves in the weeds. The girl we ask to the prom turns us down with a look that says, "Are you out of your mind?" A job doesn't work out. Someone we love dies.

We can't avoid tough times—that's just how life is. But we can choose how to respond to the tough times. Either we can be defeated by them or we can rest in the promise of God's Word that there is a purpose for what we're going through. James went even further in his view of tough times with this outrageous suggestion: "Consider it *pure joy*, my brothers, whenever you face trials of many kinds, because you know that the testing of your faith develops perseverance" (James 1:2-3, emphasis added). Joy? *Joy?* Who finds joy in the midst of their trials? It turns out there's a good example of this very thing just a little earlier in the Bible, in 2 Corinthians 8.

We want you to know about the grace that God has given the Macedonian churches. Out of the most severe trial, *their overflowing joy* and their extreme poverty welled up in rich generosity. For I testify that they gave as much as they were able, and even beyond their ability. Entirely on their own, they urgently pleaded with us for the privilege of sharing in this service to the saints. And they did not do as we expected, but they gave themselves first to the Lord and then to us in keeping with God's will. So we urged Titus, since he had earlier made a beginning, to bring also to completion this act of grace on your part. But just as you excel in everything—in faith, in speech, in knowledge, in complete earnestness and in your love for us—see that you also excel in this grace of giving. (verses 1-7, emphasis added)

Never before had I ever heard of people experiencing "severe trial" and "extreme poverty" who were also "overflowing" with joy. It just doesn't happen, right? What can account for joy in the midst of such trials? The answer, it appears, was the outward orientation of the Macedonians. They were devoted to God, and they were committed to helping others—so much, in fact, that they "urgently pleaded" for "the *privilege* of sharing" with others in need.

This may sound a bit crazy to you right now. Your circumstances may make it impossible to think of helping someone else. That's okay. Or you may be thinking that you're the last person who could help someone else. But the opposite is true. You're one of the best people who could help others. Why? Because tough times is not just a concept for you; it's not something you read about in a book. You've been there and done that.

Who Could Use Your Help?

If you will use your experience to help others, you'll have a great impact, and doing so will have a great impact on you. That's been the experience of David and April, who have learned more than their fair share of financial lessons the hard way. Early in their marriage, a small business they were involved in with David's father failed, resulting in a personal bankruptcy filing, years of a strained relationship with David's father, and much mental anguish. Later they bought a house that was too expensive for them and then furnished it with items bought on credit. They've done the math and figured out that if they had been patient and waited just a little bit longer before buying a house, they could have bought the house they live in now for cash.

April says that their involvement in a church-based stewardship ministry — that is, *serving* in the ministry — helped them get to a much better place with their finances. "Because we've given our testimony so many times, our entire church knows how we've messed up. They know that one of our goals is to pay off our home so that we can be completely debt-free. We don't have just one accountability partner; we're accountable to our entire church community."

Despite busy schedules, David and April spend many hours each week teaching financial workshops and leading a team of stewardship ministry volunteers. "We believe there's a reason for us to have gone through so much," David explained. "It's to bless someone else."

Who could you help? What about other family members, friends, neighbors, or coworkers? There are probably many people in your life who don't even know what you're going through. You don't need to put a bumper sticker on your car telling the world about your situation. But if you will take a risk and casually mention something about your situation to some of the other people in your life, you just might discover that a lot of them have financial problems too. And they just might look to you for some advice.

You could also volunteer with a financial ministry. Two good ones that you have read about in this book are Good $ense and Crown. Several thousand churches utilize Good $ense materials to teach workshops about biblical money management and counsel people one-on-one. Check out their website, www.goodsenseministry.com, for more information about Good $ense, including information about starting a Good $ense ministry at your church. For more information about getting involved in Crown, go to www.crown.org.

Seeing the Big Picture

It's been nearly twenty years since I rang up twenty thousand dollars of credit card debt and had to move back home in order to get out of debt, but I still have vivid memories of that experience. I'm glad I can remember, because when I think of the good that came from that experience, I see God's goodness with fresh eyes. That difficult period of my life was the catalyst God used to draw me into a relationship with him, and it was what helped me discover God's purpose for my life.

You probably picked up this book because you were looking for some pain relief. I pray that you have found a measure of that relief in these pages and that the ideas and stories in this book will help you get to a better place. But I also pray that your tough times will mark you for the rest of your life in a positive way—that you will look for opportunities to use your experience to help other people.

If you don't see that potential for greater impact right now, that's okay. Just keep looking and listening as you patiently take the necessary steps to resolve your financial problems. What you're going through may look like it's all about money, but I'm confident that one day you'll look back and see that it was really about so much more.

ACKNOWLEDGMENTS

M y name might be on the cover, but there are many people who contributed ideas, suggested revisions, caught mistakes, and made countless other invaluable contributions to this book.

To the Good $ense strategy team (Russ Haan, Paula Haun, Bill Hayes, John Kelley, John Onufrock, Dan Rotter, Sharon Swing, Sibyl Towner, and Jerry and Sandy Wiseman), thank you for your friendship and prayers. It's a joy to pull oars in the same ship as you.

To the leaders at Park Community Church—especially Jackson Crum, Jonathan Masters, Scott Clifton, and Bill Meier—thank you for encouraging my work.

To everyone who prayed for me or offered other forms of support while I wrote, thank you. This includes my brother, David Bell; Jim and Kirsten Bell; Paul and Sheila Jenkinson; Craig and Laurie Steensma; Bret and Becky Petkus; Dave and Emily Reuter; Jim Sharkey; Wayne Riendeau; and Tom Vislisel.

To Jim Grubb, Vivian Hayes, John Kester, David and April Schnardhorst, and Jerry Schriver, thank you for connecting me with people who have powerful stories of getting through financial tough times.

To everyone who shared your story with me, thank you for your willingness to talk so candidly. I pray that this book will help multiply the impact of your stories.

To the many experts I interviewed, thank you for your patient and helpful answers to my many questions. They include Nadiyah Casey of

Money Management International, Gail Cunningham of the National Foundation for Credit Counseling, Michele Johnson of Consumer Credit Counseling Service in Las Vegas, Pat Palmer of Medical Billing Advocates of America, and Barry Paperno of Fair Isaac Corporation.

Special thanks to Nona Ostrove. Your commitment to stewardship ministry and your expertise as a bankruptcy attorney make for a rare and powerful combination. Your ideas have had a tremendously helpful influence on my thinking, writing, and teaching.

To Robert, Erik, and Andrew Wolgemuth, and Michael Ranville, I'm honored to be represented by you. Erik, thank you for your always-sound advice, words of encouragement, and prayers.

To Liz Heaney, thank you being so amazingly good at what you do—for being so much more than an editor. It's a gift to be able to work with you.

To everyone at NavPress I've had the pleasure of meeting and/or working with—including Kathleen Campbell, Stephanie Chalfant, Jessica Chappell, Tim Frye, Eric Helus, Darla Hightower, Janet Kleeberg, Julie Langmade, Mike Linder, Pamela Mendoza, Mike Miller, Marsha Pursley, Jill Rockwell, Delbert Tuxhorn, Michael Visentine, Arvid Wallen, and Kris Wallen—thank you for the passion with which you pursue your mission. My opportunity to work with you is proof positive that God is "able to do immeasurably more than all we ask or imagine."

Especially to Dan Benson at NavPress, thank you for asking me to write this book, for your help in shaping the outline, and for your unending support. It's a privilege and a joy to work with you.

To David Briggs, the head of Good $ense at Willow Creek Community Church and one of the wisest stewardship leaders I know, thank you for your helpful comments about the manuscript. Our conversations always make me grow.

To Dick Towner, the head of Good $ense at the Willow Creek Association and another of the wisest stewardship leaders I know, thank you for your helpful feedback on the manuscript, your partnership in ministry, and your willingness to open so many doors of opportunity. Knowing you is one of my greatest blessings.

To my children, Jonathan, Andrew, and Annika. Some people listen to music while they work; I get to listen to the sound of you playing (or, in your case, Annika, cooing). It's a soundtrack that warms my heart and motivates me to do my best. Jonathan and Andrew, this book is an answer to your nightly prayers that God would "just throw open the floodgates [of opportunity] for daddy's business—tear them open really hard!" How I love hearing you guys pray. Every time a person is helped by this book is an answer to your prayers as well.

Mostly, to my wife, Jude. The opportunity to write this book coincided with the birth of our third child, and it came with an intense three-month deadline that left me disappearing into the basement to write on far too many nights and weekends. Even when we were both too tired to laugh, you responded with grace, patience, and words of encouragement. One of my strongest memories of this experience will always be the sight of you sitting at a computer, reviewing something I wrote while Annika slept on your lap. I'm so thankful to be living the adventure of life with you. The joys are more vivid, the disappointments are less painful, and my hope for the future is much greater because of you.

NOTES

Chapter 1: You *Can* Get to a Better Place

1. Stephen Arterburn and Dean Merrill, *Every Man's Bible*, New Living Translation (Carol Stream, IL: Tyndale, 2004).

Chapter 3: How Serious Are You?

1. Massachusetts Public Interest Research Group, http://www.masspirg.org/static/deflatereport.pdf.

2. "Skeptics surprised after negotiating lower credit card rate," *CBC News*, March 7, 2008, http://www.cbc.ca/consumer/story/2008/03/07/credit-cards.html.

3. Jackie Crosby, "No interest? No payments? No sympathy for the unwary," *Star Tribune*, January 7, 2007, 1D.

4. Bureau of Labor Statistics data: http://www.bls.gov/news.release/atus.t11.htm.

5. Robin Leonard and John Lamb, *Solve Your Money Troubles: Get Debt Collectors Off Your Back and Regain Financial Freedom* (Berkeley, CA: Nolo, 2007), 98.

6. Juliet B. Schor, *The Overspent American: Why We Want What We Don't Need* (New York: Basic Books, 1998), 80.

Chapter 4: "Unsecured" Debt Solutions

1. Author interview with Gail Cunningham conducted on September 3, 2008.

2. "Seeing Red: The Growing Burden of Medical Bills and Debt Faced by U.S. Families," *The Commonwealth Fund*, August 20, 2008, http://www.commonwealthfund.org/publications/publica tions_show.htm?doc_id=700868.

3. Author interview with Gail Cunningham conducted on September 3, 2008.

4. Capital One Healthcare Finance website, http://www.capitalone healthcarefinance.com/.

5. "Overdose of Debt," *Consumer Reports*, July 2008, http://www. consumerreports.org/cro/money/credit-loan/cr-investigates-medi cal-debt/overview/medical-debt-ov.htm.

6. Author interview with Pat Palmer on October 14, 2008.

7. Vanessa Fuhrmans, "Patients Seek Financial Aid to Buy Medicine," *The Wall Street Journal*, October 21, 2008, D2.

8. Tom Herman, "Wiping Out Your Tax Debt Gets Tougher," *The Wall Street Journal*, July 23, 2008, D1.

9. Robin Leonard and John Lamb, *Solve Your Money Troubles: Get Debt Collectors Off Your Back and Regain Financial Freedom* (Berkeley, CA: Nolo, 2007), 141–143.

10. http://www.ftc.gov/bcp/edu/pubs/consumer/credit/cre18.shtm.

Chapter 5: "Secured" Debt Solutions

1. Noelle Knox, "Mortgage lenders see more borrowers give up," *USA TODAY*, March 14, 2008, http://www.usatoday.com/ money/economy/housing/2008-03-09-foreclosures-walk-away_ N.htm.

2. Ruth Simon, "Easing Mortgages Isn't a Panacea," *The Wall Street Journal*, December 9, 2008, A4.

3. Author interview with Barry Paperno conducted on October 30, 2008.

4. Author interview with Michele Johnson conducted on November 21, 2008.

5. Joanne Helperin, "Get Out of Your Lease the Cheap and Easy Way," Edmunds.com, http://www.edmunds.com/advice/leasing/articles/47011/article.html.

Chapter 6: When Your Financial Engine Stops Running

1. Mary Lorenz, "Companies That Give Benefits to Part-Timers," Careerbuilder.com, http://jobs.aol.com/article/_a/companies-that-give-benefits-to-part/20070912114809990008.
2. Erin White, "Corporate Tuition Aid Appears to Keep Workers Loyal," *The Wall Street Journal*, May 21, 2007, B4.

Chapter 7: Tapping Your Reserves

1. Liz Pulliam Weston, "The 3 worst money moves you can make," *MSN*, http://articles.moneycentral.msn.com/SavingandDebt/ManageDebt/The3WorstMoneyMovesYouCanMake.aspx.
2. IRS article. http://www.irs.gov/retirement/sponsor/article/o,,id=151926,00.html.
3. Kimberly Lankford, "Cash In On Your Life," *Kiplinger's Personal Finance* magazine, July, 2008, 64–67.

Chapter 8: When All Else Fails

1. Aleksandra Todorova, "Out of Options," *SmartMoney* magazine, April 7, 2004, http://www.smartmoney.com/personal-finance/debt/out-of-options-15648/.
2. American Bar Association, *Guide to Credit & Bankruptcy*, (New York: Random House, 2006), 233.
3. "Bankruptcy Reform: Dollar Costs Associated with the Bankruptcy Abuse Prevention and Consumer Protection Act of 2005, United States Government Accountability Office, June 2008, http://www.gao.gov/new.items/d08697.pdf.
4. Author interview with Barry Paperno conducted on October 30, 2008.

5. Elisabeth Leamy, "Beware of Credit Repair," *ABC News*, October 20, 2008, http://abcnews.go.com/Business/Personal Finance/story?id=6058693&page=1.

Chapter 9: A Money Plan for Any Kind of Weather

1. *Leading the Way: A Publication of Hartford Leaders Suite of Variable Annuities Third Quarter*, 2008, 1.
2. This figure comes from an online "eNation" survey of nationally representative households I commissioned from the market research firm Synovate in October 2008.
3. Synovate eNation survey.
4. John Spence, "Buffet gives nod to index funds over EFTs," *MarketWatch*, May 7, 2007, http://www.marketwatch.com/ news/story/warren-buffett-backs-index-mutual/story.aspx ?guid=%7B4A899C35-02F6-42CB-BB01-7B7E303003D4%7D.
5. Eleanor Laise, "Statement Shock Hits 401(k)s," *The Wall Street Journal*, October 11–12, 2008, B2.
6. Kevin Lavelle, "Overcoming Loss Aversion," *Fidelity Investors Quarterly*, August 2008, 8.
7. Jonathan Burton, "The high price of panic," *MarketWatch*, November 3, 2008, http://www.marketwatch.com/News/Story/ Story.aspx?guid=6cd062f214894c79a54d1320338edadb&siteid=n whpf&sguid=XRf6VJaBX02nkePbPw8gMg.
8. "Working Longer and Other Ways to Optimize Retirement Income," June 2008, T. Rowe Price, http://www.troweprice.com/ gcFiles/pdf/2A41.pdf?scn=Articles&src=Media_Near_or_In_ Retirement&t=lgcy.
9. "7 Reasons Not to Retire." *U.S. News and World Report.* http:// www.usnews.com/usnews/biztech/articles/060612/12retire.htm.
10. In the interest of full disclosure, I am compensated by Kingdom Advisors for writing what I do for the organization.
11. Synovate eNation survey.

Chapter 10: Habits of the Heart

1. The Internet Movie Database dialogue, http://www.imdb.com/title/tt0329575/quotes.
2. *Seabiscuit* DVD, Gary Ross, dir. (Universal City, CA: Universal Studios, 2003).
3. Dr. John H. Westerhoff, *Grateful and Generous Hearts* (Atlanta: St. Luke's Press, 1997), 4–5.
4. Westerhoff, 5.
5. C. S. Lewis, *Mere Christianity* (New York: Simon & Schuster, 1996), 121.

ABOUT THE AUTHOR

MATT BELL is popular personal finance speaker and writer, director of the Willow Creek Association's national "Good $ense" stewardship ministry, and author of *Money, Purpose, Joy: The Proven Path to Uncommon Financial Success* (NavPress). His own financial tough times experience changed the direction of his life, giving him a passion to teach others how to use money for productive, joyful, God-glorifying purposes. He has been quoted in major media such as *U.S. News & World Report* and the *Chicago Tribune*.

Go deeper into discovering financial responsibility with Matt Bell!

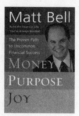

Money, Purpose, Joy
Matt Bell
978-1-60006-279-7

Discover how to connect your use of money with what matters most. In this inspiring and instructive book, financial teacher Matt Bell helps you clarify your purpose and learn a practical, biblical process for using money to fulfill that purpose.

Money, Purpose, Joy: Discussion Guide
Matt Bell
978-1-60006-322-0

Help foster life-changing discussions about money within your small group by using Matt Bell's discussion guide to *Money, Purpose, Joy.* You'll discover how to use money in ways that are more productive, satisfying, and glorifying to God.

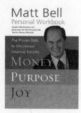

Money, Purpose, Joy: Workbook
Matt Bell
978-1-60006-321-3

Go further in your journey toward uncommon financial success with this personal workbook. The user-friendly worksheets, thought-provoking exercises, and spending guidelines will help you achieve the financial life you've always wanted.

To order copies call NavPress at 1-800-366-7788
or log on to www.navpress.com.

Willow Creek Resources

WILLOW

Willow Creek Association

Vision, Training, Resources for Prevailing Churches

This resource was created to serve you and to help you build a local church that prevails. It is just one of many ministry tools published by the Willow Creek Association.

The Willow Creek Association (WCA) was created in 1992 to serve a rapidly growing number of churches from across the denominational spectrum that are committed to helping unchurched people become fully devoted followers of Christ. Membership in the WCA now numbers over 12,000 Member Churches worldwide from more than ninety denominations.

The Willow Creek Association links like-minded Christian leaders with each other and with strategic vision, training, and resources in order to help them build prevailing churches designed to reach their redemptive potential. Here are some of the ways the WCA does that.

- **The Leadership Summit** — A once-a-year, two-day conference to envision and equip Christians with leadership gifts and responsibilities. Presented live on Willow Creek's campus as well as via satellite broadcast to over 135 locations across North America — plus more than eighty international cities via videocast — this event is designed to increase the leadership effectiveness of pastors, ministry staff, volunteer church leaders, and Christians in the marketplace.

- **Ministry-Specific Conferences** — Throughout the year the WCA hosts a variety of conferences and training events — both at Willow Creek's main campus and offsite, across North America and around the world. These events are for church leaders and volunteers in areas such as small groups, children's ministry, student ministry, preaching and teaching, the arts, and stewardship.

- **Willow Creek Resources®** — Provides churches with trusted and field-tested ministry resources in such areas as leadership, volunteer ministries, spiritual formation, stewardship, evangelism, small groups, children's ministry, student ministry, the arts, and more.

- **WCA Member Benefits** — Includes substantial discounts to WCA training events, a 20 percent discount on all Willow Creek Resources®, *Defining Moments* monthly audio journal for leaders, quarterly *Willow* magazine, access to a Members-Only section on WillowNet, monthly communications and more. Member Churches also receive special discounts and premier services through the WCA's growing number of ministry partners — Select Service Providers — and save an average of $500 annually depending on the level of engagement.

For specific information about WCA conferences, resources, membership, and other ministry services contact:

Willow Creek Association
P.O. Box 3188
Barrington, IL 60011-3188
Phone: 847.570.9812
Fax: 847.765.5046
www.willowcreek.com